DAVE & JUDY —

DREAM BIG!

HEB. 13 : 8

I MISS YOU GUYS

I DARE

— TO —

BELIEVE

GOD'S POWER
IN YOU
TO DO THE
IMPOSSIBLE

MIKE FRANCEN

To contact Mike Francen
visit www.GoFWO.org

FOGHORN
PUBLISHERS

"Of Making Many Books There Is No End..."

I Dare to Believe

ISBN-10: 1-934466-09-3

ISBN-13: 978-1-934466-09-4

Printed in Malaysia

©2008 by Michael Francen

All Rights Reserved.

Foghorn Publishers

P.O. Box 8286

Manchester, CT 06040-0286

860-216-5622

860-568-4821 fax

foghornpublisher@aol.com

—— TABLE OF CONTENTS ——

Introduction 1

1 The Grand Illusion 9

2 Don't Shop for a Canoe When God Says: Build an Ark! . 19

3 Make No Little Plans Here! 23

4 Passion and the Fire of God 35

5 A Time to Pray and a Time to Say! 45

6 Discover Your Destiny 57

7 From the Pit to the Palace 65

8 A Miracle Settles the Issue 71

9 Walk on the Water With Me 85

10 Lessons From the Book of Acts 91

11 I Give You My World 103

12 Power to Prosper 111

13 Foundation for Faith 123

14 Stone Movers/World Shakers 135

15 A Persuading Force 145

16 Seeded for Souls 153

TABLE OF CONTENTS

17 A Passion for Souls 165

18 The Pulpit Fails to Grip 179

19 Greater Works 189

20 They Shall Share Alike 203

21 It's Just the Beginning 207

22 Absolute Power 213

23 En Masse (Why I believe in mass crusade evangelism) . 223

24 Never Too Dead for a Resurrection 239

25 High Treason 249

26 Satan, a Defeated Foe 255

27 Separate Yourself 261

28 All Things Are Yours 267

29 The Good News Game 271

30 The Future is My Friend 277

INTRODUCTION

The great healing evangelist and soul winner Dr T.L. Osborn once said, "The Francens are pacesetters in the arena of world evangelism." Mike Francen's ministry personifies its statement of purpose: "Our Vision—The World! Our Passion—Souls!"

For nearly thirty years I have focused my attention, life, ministry, and energies toward reaching the nations of the world. Over that time our ministry has traveled to ninety-four countries, conducting some of the largest crusades those nations have ever had. We have freely given away tons of gospel literature and trained tens of thousands of native ministers to do the work of the ministry.

We have given ongoing support for many of those ministers, providing them with automobiles, clothing, education, office equipment, and financial support. To date we have seen more than eleven million people come to Christ in our campaigns. In many ways it seems like we are only beginning this magnificent journey, as our goal is to reach 100 million people for Christ. While we have done much thus far, in the field of mission evangelism, we are always looking for opportunities to do more for God.

FROM THE PIT TO THE PALACE

Recently I returned from the extraordinary nation of Jordan. This is the 94th nation that I have traveled to. I was totally amazed at the historical and Biblical richness of this land. The warmth and kindness of the people, their cultural heritage, and far reaching beauty puts Jordan at the top of my list of places that I must return to soon. Some of the major sights of historical value are places such as Petra, which is one of the seven man made wonders of the world, Mount Nebo, and the Dead Sea. However, the most captivating place for me was a lesser-known place called Dar Al Bir.

This story captivated my heart. Twelve years ago, the late King Hussein visited an orphanage just outside of Amman. The conditions there were barely fit for human habitation. The poverty and depraved state of the people, particularly regarding the children prompted the king to take serious action to help rectify their situation. When he returned home, back to his palace, he informed the queen that they were to immediately move out of the Palace and into the guesthouse. Moved with total compassion for the children, King Hussein moved all 200 children from the orphanage they were living into the King's Palace in less than 24 hours.

This one action from the king took these precious children from the pit to the palace. To this day, the Dar Al Bir Palace remains an orphanage. To think, that one encounter with The King, can change the course of your life in a seconds time. That gave me a newfound desire to have faith in The King on a whole new level. The world and all those that dwell in it belong to the King. How much easier would life be if you simply welcomed the King into your life and your situation and expected Him to turn things around for you?

What still amazes me about this story is that these children were living in abject poverty, and the difference between where they were and where they could be, was in the mouth of the King. I believe wholeheartedly that your life is getting ready to change just like mine did many years ago, and still continually does until this day because of one word from the King. One word from the King can change nations; it can change your financial situation, and even your health. Just be prepared to be in position to receive from the King when He speaks the Word of Destiny over your life.

FROM DRIVER TO DRIVEN

In 1984, while serving as the director of missions at a church in Minnesota, I was presented with an opportunity, which became instrumental in shaping the future of this ministry. The late Dr. Benson Idahosa, an international evangelist from Nigeria was preaching in Minnesota for a series of meetings. I was designated as the driver to take Dr. Idahosa to and from the meetings. Within the first twenty minutes of my meeting this extraordinary man, he proposed, "Son, I want you to come to Nigeria for a few months and stay at my home."

Having no idea where God was actually leading me, or what the next years of my life would be like, I dared to believe. Less than two months later I incorporated Francen World Outreach, and then found myself in Benin City, Nigeria with Dr. Benson Idahosa. Then I didn't fully realize that being in Nigeria was a major part of the training needed for the massive ministry that God would place in my hands. I accompanied Idahosa on all of his outreaches and crusades while I was there, and got the chance to learn from a remarkable man up close.

Dr. Idahosa was a man of great influence and would attract many respected ministry leaders from the United States to join him in these endeavors such as Jerry Savelle and T. L. Osborn. During the first three weeks of my stay there, I continually heard the voice of the Lord say, "Your gift will make a way for you, and bring you before great men." These words were like a constant barrage on my mind. At times I would hear the voice so strong that I would be awaken out of my sleep. It wasn't long after, that I actually heard those words so many times that it became a living part of my consciousness.

The words were engraved in my heart, "Your gift will make a way for you, and bring you before great men." God worked quickly in making this prophecy come to pass, as I began to become closer with T. L. Osborn having several opportunities to talk with him about various aspects of ministry and life in general. Sensing the anointing on my life, Dr. Osborn laid his hands on me, prayed, and began to proclaim, "You are going to do it. You are going to do it. You are going to do it." From the very outset of our first meeting God began to mesh our hearts together.

In the years that followed we would host the Osborns for three historic events in India. In the past several years we have joined forces together to conduct some of the most amazing campaigns in numerous other countries. Still in Nigeria with Idahosa, I would sit on the platform of huge crusades he was conducting, paying close attention to every detail. Tens of thousands of people would pack the grounds and phenomenal miracles happened at every service. Seeing such incredible miracles, really helped to develop my faith in God, and has given me the basis for believing God for literally everything.

As I would watch Idahosa, I began hearing God speak as before, but this time God began to say, "You can do that." As the voice increased I knew intuitively that God was prompting me to take a leap of faith toward my destiny. After spending those months in Nigeria, it was time for me to return home. My faith was inspired and my visions challenged. Before leaving Nigeria, I asked Archbishop Benson Idahosa, "Why after only twenty minutes of knowing me, did you invite me to come and stay with you in Nigeria?" He told me: "I know what God told me about your life, and you needed to learn how to do big crusades."

Curious, I asked, "Now what am I supposed to do?" Idahosa simply yet boldly said, "Son go and do likewise!" With that I headed back to the United States more driven than I have ever been in my life. I wasn't driven with my own agenda, but rather with a defined purpose and an intended aim of doing more to save souls than anyone had ever done before.

TOO YOUNG TO KNOW ANY BETTER

I have never been one to waste time, so I quickly began doing what I could to fulfill the Great Commission. I didn't have all of the answers or even a real plan of action to follow. It was God and me, and a genuine drive to make a difference. That was all I had. And of course, I had youth on my side, as I was so young that I really didn't see the obstacles that some of my elder peers saw before me. Many of my peers thought that beginning a ministry of such global reach was something much more suited for a seasoned veteran, not a kid from Cambridge, Minnesota. I was too young to know any better.

That's the advantage of being young; you aren't typically bothered by the negative comments from others, especially when you are already convinced otherwise. In December I returned from Nigeria and the very next month, January, I went to the Philippines. Imitating what I saw Idahosa do in Nigeria, I had posters and handbills printed up saying: BRING THE DEAF, BLIND, CRIPPLES. JESUS WILL HEAL THEM ALL! The people came and God healed them. None of them cared at all about my age; they wanted to receive a touch from God.

The very first night of my first ever crusade in a foreign land was filled with wonderment, excitement, as well as many questions and some serious reservations all working simultaneously. When I arrived at the crusade grounds the first night, I looked over the crowd of people there, and thought, "My God, what have I done?" Looking out over the crowd, I saw some of the sickest people that I ever seen in my entire life. There were paralytics in on stretchers. Personal guides were leading the blind into the crusade. Huge goiters and tumors protruded from the throats of elderly women.

My mind thought back to what T.L Osborn said, "You are going to do it." Suddenly I thought about the Idahosa crusades in Nigeria, when God spoke to my heart saying, "You can do that." Knowing that I had God backing me, I took the microphone and said these words, "I've not come in the name of a church. I am not here in the name of religion. I've not come in my own name. I am here in the name of the Lord Jesus Christ." I preached and prayed for the sick with boldness and conviction.

The first man to testify was a man who had been totally deaf for more than thirty-five years. There he stood totally healed by the power of God. A woman, blind for seven years wept and said, "This is the first time in seven years I have seen my grandchildren." Cripples walked and tumors disappeared. In that same crusade over 4000 people accepted Jesus and their Savior. I was too young to know any better. Imagine if the naysayers and the negative comments from the elders had discouraged me I would not be where I am today.

Thousands of sick people would have died prematurely if I didn't dare to believe. Those were the first twenty-five years. The next twenty-five years will be far greater than the first. *I Dare To Believe* is a compilation of my favorite chapters from all of the books that I've penned to date. I trust that these pages will bless, encourage, and challenge you to new levels of faith. If there has ever been a time in your life when you were told that you could not do something, this book will challenge you to DARE TO BELIEVE once again!

God Bless,
Michael Francen
Tulsa, Oklahoma 2008

CHAPTER ONE

—— THE GRAND ILLUSION ——

The greatest building has yet to be erected, the greatest invention yet to be patented. The greatest song has yet to be composed, the greatest book yet to be written. The most profound thought has yet to be perceived, the most amazing theory yet to be proven. The most beautiful poem has yet to be penned, the most powerful sermon yet to be preached. The largest church has yet to be known, the grandest victory yet to be realized. The greatest wealth has yet to be accumulated. The largest offering has yet to be given. The greatest day has yet to dawn.

> *The greatest day has yet to dawn.*

The grand illusion has been painted. Scores have purchased another's idea of success. What is the "grand illusion?"—"It's all been done; we have it all; it's not possible." Mediocrity, passivity, status quo, and average, stand and curse the limitless potential and destiny of those who would dare to soar.

In 1899 Charles H. Duell, the presiding commissioner of the U.S. Patent Office, issued this statement: *"Everything that can be invented, has been invented."* This man was chained to pettiness instead of potential. Pioneers (those who forge ahead when the common consensus is to pull back) don't see obstacles; they focus on opportunities.

Some say, "Take it easy," I say, "Take a chance." Some say, "Take care," I say, "Take charge." Some look to retire; I say "Re-fire." Courage is not the absence of fear; it is the conquering of it. When you dare to attack it, fear will then loosen its grip on you. Opportunity does not come to those who wait, rather it comes to those who attack. Those who risk nothing, gain nothing.

In defining success in life, H.G. Wells says, *"Wealth, notoriety, place, and power are no measure of success whatsoever. The only true measure of success is the ratio between what we might have done and what we might have been on the one hand, and ourselves on the other."*

In William Danforth's book, *I Dare You*, he presents this challenge:

> *"I dare you, young man, you who come from a home of poverty—I dare you to have the qualities of a Lincoln.*
>
> *I dare you, heir of wealth and proud ancestry, with your generations of worthy stock, your traditions of leadership—I dare you to achieve something that will make the future point to you with even more pride than the present is pointing to those who have gone before you.*
>
> *I dare you, young mother, to make your life a masterpiece upon which that little family of yours can build. Strong women bring forth strong men.*
>
> *I dare you, boys and girls, to make life obey you, not you it. It is only a shallow dare to do the foolish things. I dare you to do the uplifting, courageous things.*

I dare you, young executives, to shoulder more responsibility joyously, to launch out into the deep, to build magnificently.

I dare you, young author, to win the Nobel Prize.

I dare you, young researcher, to become a Microbe Hunter.

I dare you, boy on the farm, to become a master farmer—a hunger fighter.

I dare you, man of affairs, to have a 'Magnificent Obsession.'

I dare you, grandfather, with your roots deep in the soil and your head above the crowd, catching the rays of the sun, to plan a daring program to crown the years of your life.

I dare you, who think life is humdrum, to become involved. I dare you who are weak to be strong; you who are dull to be sparkling; you who are slaves to be kings."

I dare you, those who have been inspired by accolades of the Kathryn Kuhlmans and Smith Wigglesworths of the world, to soar on the edge of big. I dare you to think and dream on a scale larger than those who have paved the way.

I dare you to challenge yourself. Rise above the level of mediocrity, soar where eagles fly, take charge of YOUR world, and create it to be what you desire.

The richest place on the planet is not the diamond mines of South Africa, or the oil fields of Kuwait. The richest place on the planet is the cemetery. In the cemetery, we bury inventions never produced; ideas and dreams that never became reality; and hopes and aspirations that were never pursued.

Many take to the grave the most vibrant and explosive resource the world could ever know—God-given dreams and visions. IT'S TIME TO DREAM AGAIN!

People today poison the daring, young mind with toxic thoughts of timidity and failure. They spew venomous criticism that says, "settle down and be like everyone else." God says, "Rise up and take a stand. Dream big enough to challenge your faith." Dream big enough for God to fit into your dreams. I am not talking about being weird; I am talking about being unique. There is a difference.

When Henry Ford had need of an unbreakable glass for the windshields of his new models of cars, he refused to consult any of the experts. They knew too many reasons why no such glass could be manufactured. Ford said, *"Bring me eager young fellows who do not know the reasons why unbreakable glass cannot be made. Give this problem to ambitious young fellows who think nothing is impossible."* He got unbreakable glass.

Former President of the United States, Theodore Roosevelt was a man with vision. He said, *"I choose not to be a common man. [For] Me, it's only right to be uncommon if I can. I'll seek opportunity, not security. I do not wish to be a kept citizen—humbled and dulled by having the state look after me. I want to take the calculated risk, to dream and to build, to fail and to succeed. I'll refuse to live from hand to mouth. I'll prefer the challenges of life to the guaranteed existence, the thrill of fulfillment to the stale calm of Utopia. I will never cower before any master nor bend to any friend. It is my heritage to stand erect, proud and unafraid, to think and act for myself and face the world boldly and say, 'This I have done.'"*

In Napoleon Hill's book, *Keys To Success,* he writes: *"There is a theory which pops up again and again that the opportunities for success are fewer now than they were in the past, that our nation has reached the plateau of its success, that the world is dominated by people who already have money, and that success is a finite realm already filled to capacity. This is nothing more than a theory. There is no scarcity of opportunity. There is only a shortage of imagination... anyone who cries 'no opportunity' is simply issuing an alibi for his or her own unwillingness to assume responsibility and use imagination."*

In John Maxwell's book, *Developing the Lender Within You,* he writes *"in A Savior for All Seasons, William Barker relates the story of a bishop from the East Coast who many years ago paid a visit to a small, Midwestern religious college. He stayed at the home of the college president, who also served as professor of physics and chemistry. After dinner the bishop declared that the millennium couldn't be far off, because just about everything about nature had been discovered and all inventions conceived.*

The young college president politely disagreed and said he felt there would be many, more discoveries. When the angered bishop challenged the president to name just one such invention, the president replied he was certain that within fifty years men would be able to fly. 'Nonsense!' sputtered the outraged bishop. 'Only angels are intended to fly.'

The bishop's last name was Wright, and he had two boys at home who would prove to have greater vision than their father.

Their names were Orville and Wilbur. The father and his sons both lived under the same sky, but THEY DIDN'T HAVE THE SAME HORIZON."

The only limitations we have are the size of our dreams and the degree of our determination. Who is the man who can determine what is impossible? For the dreams of yesterday are the hopes of today—the reality of our tomorrow. Every great achievement commanding honor in the annals of the world, began as a dream. Nothing great was ever achieved without it.

Your vision is your future.

Your vision is your future. Know where you will be five years from now. The Bible says that the Holy Spirit will show us things to come. It is the knowledge of the future that gives meaning to the present. Purpose is a glimpse of the future.

So often the wealth of a dream is dashed in the poverty of discouragement. Vision transcends current setbacks and casualties in the heat of battle. Why? Because you know the end. If you don't see the end at the beginning, you cannot live your today.

Purpose is a glimpse of the future.

Many today disengage when just on the horizon lies a glimpse of the victory. Weary from the journey, an attitude begins to weave its web that says, "No matter what happens the rest of the way, this voyage has been a success." Satisfied with present attainments, they hope to coast into the finale.

A dear friend of mine once posed this thought to me, "Yesterday is history; tomorrow a mystery; and today is a gift. That is why they call it—the present." Take advantage of the present. Seize today. The best way to predict the future—CREATE IT!

The past is our teacher, the present our opportunity, and the future is our friend. People relish the past. At the turn of the century, the impact of the great Welsh and Azusa street revivals swept across the world. In the 1940s and 1950s, a healing revival caused huge tents and auditoriums to be filled to capacity. Today people long for the return of the old. We are chained to the past, too often limited to barriers and borders of our forefathers. Let us learn from the past, at the same time avoid being bound to it. God says: *"Behold, I will do a new thing"* (Isaiah 43: 18).

The best way to predict the future– CREATE IT!

Some despise the past, so they do their best to ignore, deny, or forget it. Others fear the future, so they continue soul ties to the days gone by.

I understand the Apostle Paul's purpose when he penned, *"Brethren, I do not count myself to have apprehended; but one thing [I do], forgetting those things which are behind and reaching forward to those things which are ahead"* (Philippians 3:13).

I also perceive the potent power in reflecting on past victories. Looking to the past, we can find motivation for the future. An inventory of triumphs from the past encourages us to seize the future with faith and confidence.

As a shepherd boy, David stood before Saul begging for a shot at the giant. King Saul looked upon David's youth, slight build, and inexperience and determined he had NO chance.

1 Samuel 17:34–36 records David's response: *"But David said to Saul, 'Your servant used to keep his father's sheep, and when a lion or a bear came and took a lamb out of the flock, I went out after it and struck it, and delivered [the lamb] from its mouth; and when it arose against me, I caught [it] by its beard, and struck and killed it. Your servant has killed both lion and bear; and this uncircumcised Philistine will be like one of them, seeing he has defied the armies of the living God.'"*

David looked back to previous victories and captured motivation and faith for the task at hand. He remembered God's hand with him as he battled the bear. He smiled as his mind replayed the victory over the lion. With courage and faith he would face a new foe; undaunted he claimed yet another victory. Looking to the past, he found motivation for the future.

> Now therefore, thus shall you say to My servant David, "Thus says the LORD of hosts: 'I took you from the sheepfold, from following the sheep, to be ruler over My people Israel. And I have been with you wherever you have gone, and have cut off all your enemies from before you, and have made you a name like the name of the great men who [are] on the earth.'"
>
> 1 Chronicles 17:7,8

How often they provoked Him in the wilderness,
[And] grieved Him in the desert! Yes, again and
again they tempted God, and limited the Holy One
of Israel.

They did not remember His power: The day when
He redeemed them from the enemy.

Psalm 78:40-42

George Bernard Shaw once wrote: "People are always blaming their circumstances for what they are. I don't believe in circumstances. The people who get on in this world are the people who get up and look for the circumstances they want, and if they can't find them, make them." Forget about the critics. Those who have done nothing are not qualified to judge those who HAVE done something. Don't share your 16x20 ideas with 3x5 minds.

CHAPTER TWO

DON'T SHOP FOR A CANOE WHEN GOD SAYS: BUILD AN ARK!

I don't want to play with marbles, when God says: "Move mountains." I refuse to continue to sit in the bathtub when He says: "Part the sea." And I am not going to shop for a canoe when God says: "BUILD AN ARK!"

You will never define the fullness of God's favor on your life until you venture into the impossible!

Heralded throughout the world is the common belief that we are living in the last days. Global events point towards this inevitable fact. The Gospel is a penetrating force, yet left un-proclaimed it becomes a powerless relic of history.

This marvelous world of automation has helped forge a mindset and lifestyle prone to complacency. Fast food, one hour service, and the all powerful remote control have raised our level of comfortability, while lowering our level of productivity. Creativeness has given way to the ready made.

The age old cliché—"Necessity is the mother of invention," has been all but discarded, for what is necessary anymore? The action required to fulfill the Great Commission has fallen prey to outdated and fruitless efforts. "Instant" Christianity is the current heartbeat of the body of Christ, the Gospel via satellite. In spite of the lukewarm attitude prevalent today, the Spirit of God is moving!

IT'S NEVER BEEN DONE BEFORE

I believe God is calling us to further the cause of Christ in unsurpassed measures. The global harvest is massive, and the fields are ripe. In order to facilitate the ushering in of Christ's return, we must think bigger than we have ever thought before. We must dream of grandeur never before imagined. We must dare to soar on the edge of big, in a manner that will cause the world to take notice.

God is calling us to a place that few have treaded upon. How big is your God? This place will bring you beyond yourself, into another realm of the Almighty. He is calling you to do things that you have never done before, in places where no one has ever dared try.

Moses had never delivered a million people from the hand of a powerful Pharaoh, yet God called him to do just that. Noah had never built an ark before, but he did and God used him to spare creation from obliteration. Jonah had never proclaimed deliverance to an entire city, yet we see that dramatic outcome of his belated obedience. David had never even stood before a giant, yet he delivered the head of him whom armies feared. Paul had never raised the dead before, yet the young lad falling to his death in his meeting did not close the service on a sour note. Peter had never spoken to three thousand before, yet his denial of the Savior before a simple peasant girl is but a faded memory. Philip had never been labeled a "healing evangelist" before, yet his boldness of action caused a city to give heed to his liberating message.

Reckless abandon? No. Irresponsible presumption? No. A "get your head out of the clouds" ambition? No, it is a passion that pulsates. It is an idea that has come of age. It is a focus that exalts Him. It is a relentless pursuit that borders on the edge of the insane, yet very much within the realm of possible—the realm of God. I am talking about BIG! Talking big, walking big, acting big, believing big. Great rewards await those who dare to soar on the edge of big. Maintaining the "status quo" can be left for those who embrace the mundane and the uninspiring, as their lot in life. As for my life: I refuse to shop for a canoe when God told me to build an ark!

The arena of world missions demands a new breed of missionaries. It is a form of insanity to continue to do the same things over and over and think that we will get different results.

Modern-day missions cannot continue with stale methods and vision-less strategies. Think Big!

This "BIG thinking" must not rest with those on the foreign fields alone. It is time for the SENDERS to gain a new perspective on their part. Token offerings must become a thing of the past. We are living in the last days. We are the most privileged generation who has ever inhabited this great planet. Let's make a difference as we usher in the King of Kings with a harvest of souls beyond

The arena of world missions needs you!

what anyone ever thought possible. The arena of world missions needs you!

It is this new attitude that must permeate throughout the entire body of Christ. I believe this and I am convinced of the enormous impact that could be made. Yet, I am very aware that only a small percentage will ever dare to soar on the edge of big. I am also very aware of history, and history has proven that the world can be shaped by the daring few who are chained to potential instead of pettiness. Is it possible for you to be one of the few who will be recorded in the annals of history as a pacesetter? Absolutely yes.

CHAPTER THREE

MAKE NO LITTLE PLANS HERE!

For years a sign has sat on my desk that portrays my philosophy in life: "Make No Little Plans Here!" Critics offer plenty of pessimistic thoughts when a dream from God is unveiled. Whether they are intimidated, embarrassed, or just love to be compliant to the status quo, we don't truly know their reasons for their bleak outlook concerning the dream. What we do know is that opposition to a dream is easily found. One does not have to look far to see an army of the narrow-minded being assembled. It is easy to join the ranks of the "Dr. Do Littles." The "Mr. Do Nothings" welcome members by the thousands.

Many people think I am overzealous. They feel my ambitions go beyond reason. I personally believe we need a few more people who will dare to step beyond reason. There is a fine line between faith and foolishness, yet most steer so far to the safe

You will never define the fullness of God's favor upon your life until you venture into the impossible.

side of faith they never enjoy the supernatural. I have often said, "You will never define the fullness of God's favor upon your life until you venture into the impossible."

T.L. Osborn once shared this thought with me: "I determined a long time ago to never let my ambition exceed the will of God." I embrace that theology with my whole heart. Most, however, never let the will of God stir the embers of ambition in their lives. How many lifetimes have been exhausted "waiting on God"? How many Bible school graduates will be released this year who will bury their education in a grave by simply—"waiting on God"? We must understand this one Bible fact: GOD NEVER CHANGES! (Malachi 3:6) If we desire things to be different—WE must change. Faith IS action. (James 2:17)

In recent years my ambitious goals and visionary ideas have been birthed by a revelation of Habakkuk 2:2,3 in my life. The Scripture says:

Then the LORD answered me and said: "Write the vision and make [it] plain on tablets, that he may run who reads it.

For the vision [is] yet for an appointed time; but at the end it will speak, and it will not lie. Though it tarries, wait for it; because it will surely come, it will not tarry."

PLANES, TRAINS, AND AUTOMOBILES (AND A FEW BOATS TOO!)

In the last few years, we have endeavored to expand our outreach efforts. We have witnessed amazing miracles as we have stood before the masses. Our "Quest for Souls" campaigns have allowed us to bring millions to Christ as we have seen audiences in huge fields swell to nearly 300,000 people a night.

These city-wide crusades make an awesome impact. I love the crusades; the miracles are always fresh.

In between our campaigns, we have embarked on some NEW things. While it is easy to review the results of these efforts and tag them as phenomenal successes, they were things that had never been done before, in countries no one ever would have thought possible. The infant planning stages of these outreaches were met with much skepticism as the vision was presented.

I remember our first "Train Track to Glory" project in the nation of India. This was our plan: rent an entire train, fill it with 800 Christians, and make a ten city Gospel invasion across the state of Andhra Pradesh, India. During this event we would plant and build ten churches, (providing each church with a projector and set of films, and drill a well), sow 130,000 books, give away 500,000 tracts, provide 50,000 Bibles, distribute 6,200 sets of clothes to widows and orphans, conduct a mass meeting at each of the ten stops, and more.

One of the great challenges to such an event is to secure the train. Never before had any group been allowed to rent an entire train. The train itself is government owned and operated. The government is a HINDU government. How could a Christian organization ever rent an entire train (17 cars stretching nearly 1/3 of a mile long) from a Hindu government to promote the cause of Christ? WRITE THE VISION—IT WILL SURELY COME!

Write the vision—it will surely come!

We completed the aforementioned "Train Track to Glory" project. It surpassed all of our expectations. The Hindu newspapers splashed front page headlines: GOSPEL TRAIN DRAWS MULTITUDES! We did it! Christ was exalted!

The day after the historic "Train Track to Glory" project was completed in India, we called our pastor friends in Thailand and told them of our plan to do the same in their nation. They simply laughed. "You could never do that in Thailand. The government will never allow it," they said. We have done it in Thailand as well, with even greater success. Write the vision—it shall surely come.

I had an idea to do the same thing in Peru with one exception; we would take a convoy of river boats up the Amazon, in lieu of the trains. We did it! It had never been done before, but the success of our "River of Life" tour is being heralded across South America today. Local missionaries resisted the idea. When asked why no one had ever attempted such an event before they said, "Because it is logistically impossible to do it!" Write the VISION. It shall surely come.

We recently completed our highly touted—"Invasion 2000" event in Honduras. We took a convoy of airplanes into San Pedro Sula, filled them with more than 300 ambassadors from the United States, and made a Gospel invasion in this nation. More than 12,000 people attended the Fire Conference, more than 120,000 people flooded the stadium. We rented 1,028 buses to bring people to the event. During this "Invasion 2000" event we gave away one million books. No one has ever taken a convoy of chartered airplanes on a Gospel invasion before. No one had ever rented 1,000 buses for an event before. No one has ever given away one million books at a meeting before. We made history. We sowed 6,000 of our docu-miracle films into this country. We built a church. We made front page headlines of the newspapers. The President of Honduras came to the Sunday afternoon meeting. He was shocked at our turnout (nearly 40,000 people could not even get into the packed stadium). The president said to me, "This is very, very impressive." Our budget for the event was 1.2 million U.S. dollars. When God gave us the vision, we did not have the money.

The Lord did not tell us to write the budget. He said WRITE THE VISION!!! It is time we quit making plans according to our budget and start making them according to HIS abundance.

God is calling us to do things that have never been done in places that no one has ever dared try! Behold I do a new thing.

I have a vision to plant and build 1,000 churches around the world. To date, in just a few short years, we have already built 612 of them. We will build 1,000 churches. It is written down.

Don't simply follow where the path may lead. Go where others dare not go and blaze a trail.

I will win one-hundred million people to Christ. It is written down! Write the vision—it shall surely come!

I will give tons of our books away to the hungry souls around the world. It is written. We have already freely given more than two-million of my books away.

I will sow at least 100 mobile evangelism units (vehicle and P.A. systems) into 100 different countries. It is written down—it shall surely come. At the time of this writing we have already given eighty-one mobile evangelism units.

It is simple. The Bible says, "Write the vision ...It shall surely come!" If you do not have a WRITTEN vision for your life, you do not truly believe Habakkuk 2:2–3. Grasp this promise. Prove it in your own life. Vision will create your future. Decide it today.

Don't simply follow where the path may lead. Go where others dare not go and blaze a trail.

THE POWER OF GOALS

When movement stops you become a monument. When you become satisfied, you die. With your heart and soul firmly fixed on your dreams and desires, you must learn how to formulate goals. If you never set any goals, you will never attain and fulfill them.

> **Write the vision and make it plain on tablets, that he may run who reads it.**
>
> **For the vision is yet for an appointed time; but at the end it will speak, and it will not lie. Though it tarries, wait for it; because it will surely come, it will not tarry.**
>
> Habakkuk 2:2–3

Goals turn "want to" into "do." Desire gains strength when it has concrete form. If you don't have a clear picture of what your ideal utopia will be, then what are your chances of creating it? We must start with our ultimate outcomes and then work backward, step by step.

To guide our actions on the way to achieving our dreams and visions, we must create a comprehensive, step-by-step plan. When you build a house you don't just go buy a pile of wood, nails, and tools and start hammering. When you build a house, you need a blueprint; a plan. You start with a sequence to the structure. Just as you begin with a blueprint in constructing a house, you now need to put together your own blueprint for success to attain your dreams.

Setting goals and beginning the process of working through them is translating vision into achievable, actionable doing. Using our creative imagination to visualize and conceive beyond what seems presently possible, is the dream and vision. When we set a goal we are saying, "I envision beyond what is, and I will focus my efforts to create it."

One author recorded this powerful study of goal setting, *"The difference in people's abilities to fully tap their personal resources is directly affected by their goals. A study of the 1953 graduates of Yale University, clearly demonstrates this point. The graduates interviewed were asked if they had a clear, specific set of goals written down with a plan for achieving those goals. Only three percent had written such goals. Twenty years later, in 1973, the researchers went back and interviewed the surviving members of the 1953 graduating class. They discovered that the three percent with specific written goals were worth more in financial terms than the entire 97 percent put together. Obviously, this study measures only people's financial development. However, the interviewers also discovered that the less measurable or more subjective measures, such as the level of happiness and joy that the graduates felt, also seemed to be superior in the three percent with written goals. This is the power of goal setting."*

In Casey Treat's book, *Fulfilling Your God Given Destiny* he writes: *"Destiny is a course of path in life that includes both the God-given destination you are seeking at life's end and your own faith-filled journey toward that destination."*

This description of destiny differs from some others. There are those who believe one's destiny is an act of "fate" or a result of chance. They think they have no control over their life's course or outcome. But I am here to tell you that you do! You not only have a *choice*, but a *responsibility*.

I have determined in my life that I will decide its outcome. As I mentioned earlier, the best way to predict the future is to create it! Psychics, Ouija boards, and soothsayers can peddle their nonsense elsewhere—I will fulfill my destiny.

The Roman teacher, Epictetus, once wrote, *"Tentative efforts lead to tentative outcomes. Therefore give yourself fully to your endeavors. Decide to construct your character through excellent actions and determine to pay the price of a worthy goal. The trials you encounter will introduce you to your strengths. Remain steadfast ...and one day you will build something that endures; something WORTHY OF YOUR POTENTIAL."*

RISK

In the book, *God's Little Devotional Book for Leaders,* it says:
> *"It is better to take a risk now than always live in fear."*
> *One simply cannot live without taking risks. Risk is woven into every aspect of our daily experience!*

To laugh is to risk appearing the fool.

To weep is to risk appearing sentimental.

To reach out for another is to risk involvement.

To expose feelings is to risk exposing our true self.

*To place your ideas, your dreams, before the crowd
is to risk loss.*

To love is to risk not being loved in return.

To live is to risk dying.

To hope is to risk despair.

To try at all is to risk failure.

Even so, the greatest hazard in life is to risk nothing.

The person who risks nothing:

- accomplishes nothing

- has nothing

- feels nothing

- and in the end, becomes nothing

*Don't be afraid to take calculated risk. Risk is essential
for growth in every area of life."*

As I began to share the vision of our "Invasion 2000" event in Honduras, I quickly realized the risk of such a venture. FWO (Francen World Outreach) has built a reputation of massive crusades and powerful projects during the last fifteen years. Now we would invite hundreds of our friends, supporters, and others from the United States to witness what we began to herald as a "nation shaking event." I spoke by faith, of how the magnitude of this event would command the attention of an entire nation. I proclaimed the vision for months prior to "Invasion 2000." The risk was great. Millions of people, in 54 countries, would be watching the

> *To risk nothing is to gain nothing.*

live television broadcast of the event. A thousand things could have gone wrong. In crusade evangelism there is no guarantee of a huge crowd. We risked our reputation. We risked a huge financial investment into the event. We risked failure. We risked embarrassment. To risk nothing is to gain nothing. We took a risk—we reaped a mighty harvest in Honduras. We took a risk—and "Invasion 2000" exceeded all of our expectations. Destiny is not a matter of chance, it is a matter of choice. I choose to create my own destiny.

In Peter Bernstein's book, *Against the Gods,* he writes: *"The revolutionary idea that defines the boundary between modern times and the past is the mastery of risk: the notion that the future is more than a whim of the gods and that men and women are not passive before nature. Until human beings discovered a way*

> *I choose to create my own destiny.*

across that boundary, the future was a mirror of the past or the murky domain of oracles and soothsayers who held a monopoly over knowledge of anticipated events... The word "risk" derives from the early Italian risicare, which means "to dare." In this sense, risk is a choice rather than fate. The actions we dare to take, which depend on how free we are to make choices, are what the story of risk is all about."

DETERMINED

Former President Theodore Roosevelt once said, *"It is not the critic who counts, not the person who points out where the doer of deeds could have done better. The credit belongs to the person who is actually in the arena; whose face is marred by dust and sweat and blood; who strives valiantly; who errs and comes up short again and spends himself or herself in a worthy cause; who at best knows in the end the triumph of high achievement; and at the worst, at least fails while daring greatly; so that his or her place shall never be with those cold and timid souls who know neither victory nor defeat."*

Some people succeed because they are destined to, most however succeed because they are determined to.

Abraham Lincoln's life personified perseverance. He failed in business in 1831. He was defeated for state legislation in 1832. He tried and failed at another business in 1833. His fiancée died in 1835.

> *Some people succeed because they are destined to; most, however, succeed because they are determined to.*

He had a nervous breakdown in 1836. In 1843 he ran for Congress and was defeated. In 1848 he tried again and was defeated. He tried running for the Senate in 1856—he lost. The next year he ran for vice-president and was defeated. In 1859 he ran once again for Senate and lost. In 1860, the man who signed his name A. Lincoln, was elected the 16th President of the United States!

Calvin Coolidge once said: *"Nothing in the world can take the place of persistence. Talent will not; nothing is more common than unsuccessful men with talent. Genius will not; unrewarded genius is almost a proverb. Education will not; the world is full of educated derelicts. Persistence and determination alone are omnipotent."*

> *A ship in the harbor is safe, but that is not why a ship was made.*

A ship in the harbor is safe, but that is not why a ship was made. Dare to dream. Dare to soar on the edge of big. Dare to blaze new trails. Dare to speak when the common stay silent. Dare to act when the timid stand motionless. Dare to imagine when the majority cast them down.

Put a sign across the borders of your mind that states:

"MAKE NO LITTLE PLANS HERE!"

CHAPTER FOUR

PASSION AND THE FIRE OF GOD

You must harbor a passion to champion a cause. Vision without passion takes on an almost whimsical state. Vision without passion is a mere puff in the wind in the face of adversity. Vision without passion will go to the grave as merely a "good idea."

Vision without passion will go to the grave as merely a "good idea."

The movers and shakers who shape our world all possess a common quality that catapults them ahead of the crowd on their way to achieving their accolades. Each possesses an inalienable burning passion to attain their visionary ideas.

Driven, excessive, narrow-minded, and consumed are adjectives ascribed to these firebrands. But it is the man with a vision, touched by the fire of God, and consumed with a passion to fulfill the vision who will always bear the brunt of the critic's tongue.

What is passion? According to Webster's dictionary it is defined as: zeal, ardor, vehement desire. Why passion? It provides the motivating force which gives life to vision. Passion can empower us to literally transcend fear, doubt, and the discouragement that will try to rise as a foe in our quest. The passion behind vision brings a deep energy and boldness to the forefront of our lives.

The key to motivation is motive. It is the why behind the vision. The reason that some people fail is not due to lack of vision, but lack of resolve. Great minds have purpose, while others have wishes.

It was the passion behind vision that caused John Wesley to: travel 250,000 miles on horseback (averaging 20 miles a day for forty years), preach 40,000 sermons, produce 400 books, and learn ten languages. At 83 years of age he was annoyed that he couldn't write more than fifteen hours a day without straining his eyes.

Great minds have purpose, while others have wishes.

At 86 he was ashamed that he could not preach more than twice a day and in his diary wrote he had developed a tendency to want to lie in bed until 5:30a.m. This man's life bore the fruit of vision coupled with passion.

Passion changed Paul and Silas into a dynamic duo that "turned the world upside down." (Acts 17:6)

Passion bred boldness in Peter and John so that when people "saw the boldness of Peter and John, and perceived that they were unlearned and ignorant men, they marveled; and they took knowledge of them, that they had been with Jesus."

THE TOUCH OF FIRE

The fire of God brings commitment to the cause. The fire of the world seeks the comfort and acceptance of man.

Peter is portrayed as two different types of a man in the gospels. The first Peter sought the fire of the world.

> But Peter said to Him, "Even if all are made to stumble, yet I will not be."
>
> And Jesus said to him, "Assuredly, I say to you that today, even this night, before the rooster crows twice, you will deny Me three times."
>
> But he spoke more vehemently, "If I have to die with You, I will not deny You!"
>
> Mark 14:29-31

> Now as Peter was below in the courtyard, one of the servant girls of the high priest came.
>
> And when she saw Peter warming himself, she looked at him and said, "You also were with Jesus of Nazareth."
>
> But he denied it, saying, "I neither know nor understand what you are saying." And he went out on the porch, and a rooster crowed.
>
> And the servant girl saw him again, and began to say to those who stood by, "This is one of them."
>
> But he denied it again. And a little later those who stood by said to Peter again, "Surely you are one of them; for your speech shows it."
>
> But he began to curse and swear, "I do not know this Man of whom you speak!"
>
> Mark 14:66-71

The fire of the world is uncommitted and un-confrontational. The fire of the world thrives on comfort. Even a little servant girl sent Peter into a panic. If you don't stand for something, you will fall for anything.

After being touched by the fire of God we are shown a totally rejuvenated Peter. The passion of God, spawned by the touch of His fire, transformed him into a formidable force who is touted as an example of faith and boldness personified.

Passion will see your dream through the difficult times.

The Peter filled with vision and backed with passion, who previously could not confess Christ in front of one little servant girl, now stood in the midst of three thousand people and brought them to the foot of the cross. When he was brought before the Sanhedrin and should have feared for his life, he said, "We ought to obey God rather than man." To shut him up, the passion-filled Peter had to be beheaded. Your God-given dream must be touched by the fire of God, for it is in the Master's kiln that passion is born.

Most revel in their comfort zones, but you must get out of the boat if you ever want to walk on the water. The flags of all your tomorrows have sailed at half mast. It is time to raise them once again!

Passion will see your dream through the difficult times. Passion will drive you forward when conventional wisdom says retreat and regroup. Compromise gives way to passion even in the tempestuous times. In the leanest of financial hardships, passion sees the entrepreneur's vision to finance the propagation of the gospel to the entire world.

PASSION POSTS ITS REWARD

Recently we conducted a crusade in the war torn nation of Liberia. I have a dream to bring the gospel of Jesus Christ to the dark corners of the world. Passion causes me to go where others "feel led not to go."

Most airlines would not, nor could not, fly into Monrovia, Liberia. For years the nation has been at war. The international airport was under siege and a great deal of damage was done to the extent that planes could no longer land there. Rebels lurked near the landing strip.

A secondary airfield, which could handle the small Russian aircraft, was used. The warlords and rebels tainted the countryside; it was a nation under great distress. Shell shocked buildings and vehicles were everywhere. Wisdom says, "Come back at another time." Passion drives you to face adversity and claims the victory.

We met with the President of the country and he offered sincere appreciation for our coming. He said, "Everyone is waiting for the war to stop before they will come to help, but you came at a dangerous time. You have told our people you care."

The fruit of vision and passion posted its reward. The Liberia campaign drew crowds in excess of 100,000 people, the largest gathering the nation has ever seen. The national government radio station broadcasts the campaign, live every day across the entire nation. Millions tuned in daily. The newspapers carried front-page headlines and miracle pictures as well as center spreads. An incredible harvest of souls came to know Christ.

Eight days after the Monrovia campaign, the mayor of the city called me from Africa stating, "Since the close of the campaign my home and office has been inundated with calls and visits of our people desperately seeking your return. Please come back any time you possibly can this year."

Reports have come back to us that even three months after the crusade the advertisement posters still remained. No one would allow them to be removed, as it was a memorial of God's visitation upon their nation.

BROKEN FOCUS

One magazine article describes what happens when people lose their vision. A group of pilgrims landed on the shores of America about 370 years ago. With great vision and courage they had come to settle in the new land. In the first year, they established a town. In the second, they elected a town council. In the third, the government proposed building a road five miles westward into the wilderness. But in the fourth year, the people tried to impeach the town council because the people thought such a road into the forest was a waste of public funds. Somehow these forward looking people had lost their vision. Once able to see across oceans, they now could not look five miles into the wilderness.

Stop living to impress people and live before God. People tell God THEIR plan and expect God to make it happen, and get mad at Him when He doesn't. God is the author and finisher. He is not required to finish anything that he did not author.

Often a double standard is set forth by pastors of churches. Wanting to add to their repertoire of many talents, well-meaning pastors decide it is their duty to step into the evangelist's role and anointing. Thus he ventures overseas to minister to the masses. Many toss great sums of money into these efforts, with little fruit for the investment. Void of passion for the task, many are doomed to fizzle without setting the nation ablaze for God.

Criticism is heard from the church platforms spouting off that the evangelist who starts a church is missing God. Yet all the while they commit the same offense—stepping beyond their anointing desiring to do *good things*.

Some pastors are going to the foreign soils and conducting successful campaigns. But these same ones are doing it at home because it is part of their God-given dream.

Broken focus thwarts and drains the very life out of vision.

Broken focus thwarts and drains the very life out of vision. Unrealized dreams eat away at the very life of a man's spirit. You are living an illusion if you are so naive as to think that the world will stand and applaud your dream. The potent power of passion enables you to stand alone in the quest of fulfilling your dream.

I have witnessed the diluted effectiveness of broken focus. As well meaning as the intentions are behind the act, we must remain focused on the dream God has placed in our own hearts.

A classic example is the host of churches across the land who adopted the cell group concept made popular by Paul Yonggi Cho of Korea. Many pastors "tried" the idea in their own congregations. Frustration soon set in and they aborted the plan as quickly as they adopted it.

Why did the concept not work for many of the well meaning pastors? Lack of passion. They took an idea, a dream someone else was given to do and tried to make it their own, thus passion eluded them.

How can we know if the dream we pursue is from God? It is from Him if: 1) You cannot let it go. 2) The dream is bigger than you. 3) You are willing to give your life to it and for it. 4) You treat it like you do God.

LOOK ON US

The media has declared open season on ministries today. The adversity they pose has made many in ministry today skittish and timid. "Don't look at me" is the plea of many ministers as they hope to avoid the scrutiny of the devourers. No one seeks to take any responsibility in this sue-crazed society.

But God says we are a city set on a hill. We are instructed to let our light shine. A man or woman touched with the fire and passion of God, who knows where he or she is going, boldly proclaims as Peter and John did, "Look at us."

On my desk there is a plaque that reads: **Make No Little Plans Here**. Vision is encapsulated in the statement. I am not going to play with marbles when God told me to move mountains.

Passion will take the vision of a man and transport it into the reality of the day. Seek the touch of the fire of God upon your life and God-given dream.

GET STARTED NOW

I once read this potent allegory. It is the story of how the devil wanted to destroy the world. He called his chief assistants. First came Anger, who said, "Let me go and destroy man. I will set brother against brother. I will get men angry with each other and they will destroy themselves."

Next spoke Lust. "I will defile men's minds. I will make love disappear and men will be turned into beasts." Then Greed said, "Allow me to go and I will instill in men's hearts the most destructive of all passions. Man's own uncontrolled desires will destroy him."

The twins, Gluttony and Drunkenness, came and told how they could make men's bodies diseased and their minds besotted. Envy, Jealousy, and Hate each told how he could destroy man. Idleness claimed he could do the job.

But with none of these was the devil satisfied. Finally, his last assistant came in. This one said, "I shall talk to man persuasively in terms of all that God wants him to be. I shall tell him how fine his plans are to be honest, clean and brave. I shall encourage him in the good purposes of his life."

The devil was aghast at such talk, But the assistant continued, "However, I shall tell man there is no hurry, he can do all of those things tomorrow. I shall advise him to wait until conditions become more favorable before he starts."

The devil replied, "You are the one who shall go on earth to destroy man." It was Procrastination—just put it off a little longer.

> He was going to be all a mortal should be, tomorrow;
>
> No one should be braver or kinder than he, tomorrow;
>
> The greatest of workers this man would have been, tomorrow.
>
> But the fact is, he died and faded from view,
>
> And all that he left here when living was through
>
> Was a mountain of things he intended to do,
> **TOMORROW**.

Begin the passionate pursuit of your vision today. Tomorrow never comes. Get started. **NOW** spelled backwards is **WON**!

CHAPTER FIVE

A TIME TO PRAY AND A TIME TO SAY!

Few people fully understand the power of words, yet while Jesus was here on the earth, He operated in this faith principle, which is found in Mark 11:23:

> **For assuredly, I say to you, whoever says to this mountain, "Be removed and be cast into the sea," and does not doubt in his heart, but believes that those things he says will come to pass, he will have whatever he says.**

Jesus spoke words and with them calmed the wind and the seas! He spoke words and made blind eyes open and deaf ears hear! When Jesus spoke words, the dead were raised, and demons fled!

Power and the creative ability of God are in our words, too.

Do you know there is not one account recorded in the Book of Acts where the apostles prayed for someone to be healed?

Power and the creative ability of God are in our words.

They did not pray for the sick; they spoke to the sick and commanded power!

When Jesus sent His disciples to teach and preach in the cities of ancient Palestine, He did not tell them to go and pray for the sick to be healed. He said, *"Go and heal the sick!"* (Matthew 10:7–8).

How were the disciples supposed to "heal the sick?" It was not through some power of their own. It was through their words, that, when spoken, *released the power of God.*

In Acts 3:1–8 we read of the powerful account of Peter and John as they encountered the crippled man:

> Now Peter and John went up together to the temple at the hour of prayer, the ninth hour.
>
> And a certain man lame from his mother's womb was carried, whom they laid daily at the gate of the temple which is called Beautiful, to ask alms from those who entered the temple; who, seeing Peter and John about to go into the temple, asked for alms.
>
> And fixing his eyes on him with John, Peter said, "Look at us."
>
> So he gave them his attention, expecting to receive something from them.
>
> Then Peter said, "Silver and gold I do not have, but what I do have I give you: In the name of Jesus Christ of Nazareth, rise up and walk."
>
> And he took him by the right hand and lifted him up, and immediately his feet and ankle bones received strength.
>
> So he, leaping up, stood and walked and entered the temple with them—walking, leaping, and praising God.

Peter did not pray He did not fast. He did what he was told to do: He spoke with authority and commanded the sick to be healed! And it was as he spoke that the miracle came.

Another account of speaking healing is found in Acts 9:36–41:

> At Joppa there was a certain disciple named Tabitha, which is translated Dorcas. This woman was full of good works and charitable deeds which she did.
>
> But it happened in those days that she became sick and died. When they had washed her, they laid her in an upper room.
>
> And since Lydda was near Joppa, and the disciples had heard that Peter was there, they sent two men to him, imploring him not to delay in coming to them.
>
> Then Peter arose and went with them. When he had come, they brought him to the upper room. And all the widows stood by him weeping, showing the tunics and garments which Dorcas had made while she was with them.
>
> But Peter put them all out, and knelt down and prayed. And turning to the body he said, "Tabitha, arise." And she opened her eyes, and when she saw Peter she sat up.
>
> Then he gave her his hand and lifted her up; and when he had called the saints and widows, he presented her alive.

We are not told to pray and fast to set people free from sickness or demons—*we are to speak the Word! Faith-filled words release the creative ability and power of God on the earth!*

I am not advocating that we should not pray. What I am stating is this: There is a time to pray, and there is a time to say. There is a time to petition the Father, and there is a time to speak forth His power. There is a time to let your requests be known to God, and there is a time to command sickness, demons, and mountains to go!

Jesus is the one who said, *"Whoever says to this mountain..."* He did not tell us to pray our mountains away.

Pastor Alex prayed for five years for his son to be healed, but nothing changed. Then the Holy Spirit spoke to his heart and told him to *tell* his son to "walk and talk." He began speaking to his mountain, and that mountain was removed in just a few months' time.

There is a time to *pray* and there is a time to say.

Before Jesus ascended back to the Father, He appeared to His disciples one last time and said, *"All authority has been given to Me in heaven and on earth. Go therefore..."* (Matthew 28:18,19).

Jesus conferred (or delegated) authority back to His Church. You and I are the Church today. We have the authority to operate and act just like Jesus did while He was here on earth, because He has given us His authority.

Now we must begin to use our authority here on this earth. The way we operate in and use our delegated authority is *by our words.*

Kenneth E. Hagin tells about an experience he had in prayer. While he was praying, an imp got between Rev. Hagin and Jesus and caused such a disturbance, jumping up and down and yelling, that Brother Hagin could not hear what Jesus was saying.

Brother Hagin waited for some time, expecting Jesus to do something about it. After a while, it became apparent that Jesus was not going to do anything about the demon, so Brother Hagin took authority over it and it left.

Then Jesus spoke to Brother Hagin and said, "If you had not done this, I could not have done it." Jesus went on to explain that He could not bind Satan, because He had given that power and authority to the believer.

You see, when He went to the cross, Jesus gave all power and authority over the devil to the Church. Jesus said:

> ...**on this rock** (the confession of Jesus' Lordship) **I will build my Church, and the gates of Hades shall not prevail against it.**
>
> **And I will give you the keys of the kingdom of heaven, and whatever you bind on earth will be bound in heaven, and whatever you loose on earth will be loosed in heaven.**
>
> Matthew 16:18-19

Most people have never realized this. They continue to ask God to do something about the devil, but Jesus has already done all He is going to do about the devil! He has already won the victory over the devil. The devil is eternally defeated.

We believers have authority on the earth. We can walk on the earth in the same manner Jesus did. *Our authority is demonstrated through our words.* The way we reign over demons is by our words! Sickness and demons have to flee at our words! Mountains will be removed by our faith-filled words!

The creative ability of God is within us. The power of God is loosed when we speak faith-filled words. God's Word is creative power. That creative power is produced by the heart, formed by the tongue, and released out of the mouth by words. For the Word to be effective, man must speak it in faith.

God's Word is not void of power; His people are void of speech. Thus, the Word is powerless only when it is unspoken.

> **Thou shalt also decree a thing, and it shall be established unto thee...**
>
> Job 22:28

There is a time to agree in prayer, and there is a time to decree in prayer. Speak the Word of God. There is a miracle in your mouth!

Once while I was holding a crusade in Kampala, Uganda, I was invited to preach at one of the tremendous overnight prayer meetings at the Miracle Centre church. These prayer meetings are attended by 4,000 to 6,000 people.

God's Word is not void of power; His people are void of speech. Thus, the Word is powerless only when it is unspoken.

That night, I preached a message on the very title of the book, "A Miracle in Your Mouth."

I told the people that there is a time to pray, and there is also a time to say. I told them you cannot pray for sickness to go; instead, you *command* sickness to go in Jesus' Name.

After I had preached, we began to command and decree sickness and demons to go. As we began to speak the Word, everyone could feel the power of God begin to fill that church.

I then asked all who were healed to raise their hands. Immediately hundreds of people raised their hands, claiming they were instantly healed.

One old man came walking up to the platform with his wife and daughter. His wife tearfully began to testify that her husband had not been able to walk or talk for nine years. When we began to speak to the mountains, his mountain of paralysis was removed, and he stood up and began to walk.

As he strutted back and forth across the stage, the crowd became "electrified" with this miracle. When I put the microphone up to his mouth, his tongue was loosed, and he spoke plainly for the first time in nine years. His mountain was removed!

This man had been prayed for many times. It was when we began to speak to his mountain that it was removed. God said, *"decree a thing, and it shall be established unto thee."* Job 22:28

T.L. Osborn begins the first chapter of his book, *Faith Speaks,* with these great truths:

"You said you could not do it; and the moment you said it you were whipped.

You said you did not have faith; at that moment doubt arose like a giant and bound you.

You talked failure and failure held you in bondage.

You talked fear and fear increased its grip on you.

Perhaps you never realized it, but to a great extent you are ruled by your words."

Solomon said:

> You are snared by the words of your own mouth; You
> are taken by the words of your mouth.
>
> Proverbs 6:2

James said that our tongue *"sets on fire the course of nature"*
(James 3:6).

Solomon further states:

> ...But the mouth of the upright will deliver them.
> A man will be satisfied with good by the fruit of
> his mouth...
>
> Proverbs 12:6

> A man's stomach shall be satisfied from the fruit of
> his mouth, and from the produce of his lips he shall
> be filled.
>
> Proverbs 12:14

> Death and life are in the power of the tongue, and
> those who love it will eat its fruit.
>
> Proverbs 18:20–21

Life or death is your choice. It is in the power of your tongue.
The words you speak can put you over in life, or they can cause
destruction. Your words may lift you up or plot your demise. We are
ruled by our words more than most of us realize. Our words can
deliver us, or they can put us into bondage. (See Matthew 12:37).

We have bound ourselves by the words of our mouths, and
then we blame God because deliverance has not come.

You cannot ask God to prosper you when your words are constantly speaking poverty! Just as you can bind the devil with your words, you can bind the blessings of God from overtaking you with your words.

> *Life or death is your choice. It is in the power of your tongue.*

When you speak Satan's words out of your mouth—words of sickness, poverty, and defeat—you are establishing his authority in your life.

You may very well be where you are today in life because of the confession of your mouth. Be encouraged by the fact that you can speak forth life, and blessings will come.

Remember, the words of your mouth have creative power, and they will create either good or evil. Let's look at some examples of this.

In Matthew 9, we read where the woman with the issue of blood said, *"...If only I may touch His garment, I shall be made well"* (verse 21). And Jesus said to her, *"Be of good cheer, daughter; your faith has made you well"* (verse 22). She received what she believed and *said!*

You can have what you say. When I was scheduled to have all four of my wisdom teeth pulled, I was told that I would have a great deal of pain afterwards.

As I drove to the dentist for my appointment, I *said,* "I will not have any pain, because Jesus bore my pain." I had no pain whatsoever, either during the procedure or afterwards. You can have what you say! There is a miracle in your mouth—speak it out!

In Numbers 13:17–33, we read the story of the 12 spies who were sent across Jordan to spy out the Promised Land. Notice verses 30 and 31:

> Then Caleb quieted the people before Moses, and said, "Let us go up at once and take possession, for we are well able to overcome it."
>
> But the men who had gone up with him said, "We are not able to go up against the people, for they are stronger than we."

All 12 of the spies got exactly what they *said*. Joshua and Caleb *said, "We are well able to overcome it"* (Numbers 13:20). They got what they said. They were the only two out of that entire generation to enter in and possess the Promised Land.

The other 10 spies said, *"...if only we had died in this wilderness!"* (Numbers 14:2) They got what they said, too. They died in the wilderness!

> Let us hold fast the confession of our hope (faith) without wavering, for He who promised is faithful.
>
> Hebrews 10:23

What is the confession we are to hold fast? It is the confession of God's Word. The word "confession" in the Greek means "saying the same thing as." So we are to say what God says. Agree with and say His Word.

We are to confess the promises of God in the face of contrary evidence and circumstances. I'm not referring to "positive thinking" or "mind over matter" here; I'm referring to speaking forth God's eternal Word.

In the face of adversity, poverty, or sickness, we should go to God's Word, which is His promise. Then you have to make a choice, because the Bible says that *"all the promises of God in him are yea, and in him Amen ..."* (2 Corinthians 1:20).

You can begin to confess (or say the same thing as) what the devil is saying to you: "I am sick and getting worse." "I will never get out of debt." "It will never work for me."

Or you can begin to confess or say the same thing as God says: "By His stripes I am healed." "My God shall supply all of my needs according to His riches in glory." "In all things I am more than a conqueror."

Again, the Bible says that death and life are in the power of your tongue, and you are taken by the words of your mouth.

Our confessions should center around these five things:

First, what Jesus has wrought for us in His death, burial, and resurrection.

Second, what has been given to us in the New Birth and the baptism in the Holy Spirit.

Third, who we are in Christ.

Fourth, what Jesus is doing for us at this present time.

Fifth, what God's Word spoken from our mouths can do.

The Apostle Paul wrote:

> ...The Word is near you, even in your mouth and in your heart (that is, the word of faith which we preach):
>
> That if you confess with your mouth the Lord Jesus and believe in your heart that God raised Him from the dead, you will be saved.

For with the heart one believes to righteousness, and with the mouth confession is made unto salvation.

Romans 10:8-10

How does the miracle of salvation come? By your words—by your confession! The miracle is in your mouth. There is a miracle in your mouth! Speak it forth. Confess the Word. The power is in the Word of God, but the power of the Word is released only when it is spoken.

The power is in the Word of God.

The power that comes from confessing the Word of God is also recognized in the Old Testament, as we see from this verse in the first chapter of Joshua:

> This Book of the Law shall not depart from your mouth, but you shall meditate in it day and night, that you may observe to do according to all that is written in it. For then you will make your way prosperous, and then you will have good success.

Joshua1:8

The power and the creative ability is in the Word. The miracle release of that power is in your mouth. Confess (say the same thing as) the promises of God.

Decree that all of your debts are paid. Confess that Jehovah-Jireh is your provider. Speak to your mountain and it will go!

There is a miracle in your mouth!

CHAPTER SIX

DISCOVER YOUR DESTINY

Alfred Nobel was a gifted man of great talents and stark contrasts. Although he is most commonly known, and has earned lasting fame today, as the founder of the "Nobel Peace Prize," this multi-millionaire is credited with patents on more than 300 inventions. Nobel would go on to have 80 companies in 20 different countries.

In 1863 Nobel succeeded in exploding nitroglycerine. Soon he had established factories in Sweden, Germany, and the United States for manufacturing the explosive. In 1865 Nobel invented the mercury fulminate detonator, the basis of all future high explosives. Two years after that he patented the more stable dynamite (this invention would quickly make him one of the worlds wealthiest men). Later his inquiries would lead Nobel to discover ballistite, a projectile propellant that became widely used by the military.

In 1888 Nobel read his own obituary in a newspaper. The obituary had been written by a journalist who had confused him with his brother. The contents of the obituary was a great shock to Nobel, not only because he was presumed dead, but because for the first time in his life he became aware of how the world viewed him. He was thought of as the man who amassed great wealth through his invention of dynamite and weapons of mass destruction, even though his inventions were only intended for use in mining and road construction.

Upon reading his own mistaken obituary, Nobel decided to change public perception—thus his destiny. He set out to show the world his heartfelt longing and ideals for global peace. He left the bulk of his massive estate to endow annual prizes to those who had most benefited the world in one of the following subjects: physics, chemistry, medicine, literature, and peace.

A man who became wealthy as a result of his inventions that brought mass destruction, stands famous today as the world's most symbolic stand for peace—The Nobel Peace Prize. Nobel determined his own destiny!

IDENTITY AND PURPOSE MEET

The story of Josiah, told in the book of Kings, gives us a biblical account of another man who discovered, and ultimately determined, his destiny.

> Josiah was eight years old when he became king, and
> he reigned thirty-one years in Jerusalem. His mother's
> name was Jedidah the daughter of Adaiah of Bozkath.
> And he did what was right in the sight of the LORD,
> and walked in all the ways of his father David; he did
> not turn aside to the right hand or to the left.
>
> 2 Kings 22:1-2

The chapters prior to this passage give us a vivid picture of the spiritual state of Jerusalem. Idolatry, male prostitution abounded, and sin ran rampant. Yet in the midst of spiritual darkness, God raised up a young man with a heart tender towards heaven—Josiah.

Even though God anointed Josiah king, even though he did that which was "right" in the sight of the Lord, I would submit to you that something was missing in his life! Possibly no other portrait of a biblical character so parallels the condition of the average Christian in America today. Josiah was a good, God-fearing, man.

His heart tender towards the Father.

His heart tender towards the Father. He was a decent king living in a corrupt nation.

Like Josiah, many today are converted, faithful, and aware, yet something missing. Josiah's hunger to please God sent him on a quest to serve. One day Josiah decided to renovate the temple which had begun to show the years of wear and neglect. Carpenters and masons were assembled and the work commenced. Daily reports were brought back to Josiah as to the progress of operation "Temple Renovation." In the midst of the temple renovation a scroll was found -

> Then Hilkiah the high priest said to Shaphan the scribe, "I have found the Book of the Law in the house of the LORD!" And Hilkiah gave the book to Shaphan, and he read it. So Shaphan the scribe went to the king, bringing the king word, saying, "Your servants have gathered the money that was found in the house, and have delivered it into the hand of those who do the work, who oversee the house of the LORD." Then Shaphan the scribe showed the king, saying, "Hilkiah the priest has given me a book!" And Shaphan read it before the king. Now it

happened, when the king heard the words of the Book of the Law, that he tore his clothes.

2 Kings 22:8-11

Upon reading the words of the scroll that was found, Josiah tore his clothes and made a radical change. In a week's time he revolutionized Jerusalem. Idols, spiritists, and abominations were destroyed (2 Kings 23:24). Prostitutes were put out and lawlessness defied. No longer was he merely a convert, now he was consumed. He moved from being simply faithful to fiery. Now Josiah was not just "aware" of the sin that abounded, he was awakened to it. No more just a heart of inspiration, now a heart of desperation.

What could one man possibly have read that would cause him to make such a radical change? What words could stir a man's heart that would result in his actions bringing widespread revival?

The life changing words read in that scroll that day was a prophecy given more than three hundred years before Josiah was even born. I Kings 13 reveal the words that said in essence, "Josiah would restore Jerusalem." JOSIAH SAW HIS NAME IN THE BOOK!!! Suddenly he saw his identity and purpose. Suddenly he discovered his DESTINY!

It is the fusion of identity and purpose that will launch you into your destiny.

YOUR name is in the book! Your purpose for existence is revealed in the pages. As you hold the Holy Word and see your name and purpose on its pages you will discover your destiny. In a moment's time your life can be revolutionized.

Even Jesus understood the potent force of identity, purpose, and destiny:

And beginning at Moses and all the Prophets, He expounded to them in all the Scriptures the things concerning Himself.

Luke 24:27

I HAVE A DREAM

History is not a divine force set in stone; it is the servant of those who make it. This liberating idea makes room for us to dream once again. Stale methods and ideologies have always given way to the dreamers of their day.

The dream became their rally cry.

In 1963, Martin Luther King delivered a speech that reverberated around the world. The "I Have a Dream" speech has been a catalyst that has helped bring King's dream to the borders of reality. His premature and untimely death could not persuade the dream to die, for it was too late. The dream had already taken on a life of its own. The dream of this man had gathered the support of many who were like-minded.

The dream became their rally cry.

Today, we see how far this dream has come. Although some would contend the content of King's dream is far from realized, no one can dispute the great strides that have been made towards its fulfillment.

The annals of history reveal a world that has been shaped and forged by the dreamers of that day. The few who dare to dream in spite of the critic's tongue are the ones who shape their generation.

Henry Ford, Benjamin Franklin, Wilbur Wright, and Albert Einstein were dreamers. Most in their day scoffed at their ideas, failing to see, yet, the world today applauds their achievements and are thankful for their dreams.

Over the centuries, God has spawned the seed of a dream within men and women and used them to impact their world. Viewing the Bible as a history book, we look at the dreams and accomplishments of Joseph, Moses, or David, and acknowledge they were used by God in a mighty way. When taking the Bible merely as a history book, no thought of personal accolades ever enters one's heart.

Taking the Bible as God's Word, drawing inspiration and hope from its pages, gives us a foundation to believe in our dreams, a platform to dream bigger than we have ever dared, and the confidence to actually realize those dreams.

TIME

Waiting for life to unveil its plan, too many sit idly by and adopt another's idea. In people's attempt to "kill time," they are doing nothing more than "wasting time." Time is a force which cannot be "killed," it passes regardless of what arsenal is amassed against it. The only thing put to death is opportunity. Everyone is allotted the same amount of time, no more, no less. Sixty minutes in an hour, twenty-four hours in a day, seven days in a week.

Time cannot be altered or stolen. It faces us as possibly the most valuable commodity one could ever have. Yet with the absolute value of this precious gem, many spend too much time wasting time. The only way for you to get more time, is to use someone else's. Learn to delegate so that your time may be used to its fullest. Take the time to search the scriptures and see your identity and purpose, and ultimately you will discover your destiny.

The only way for you to get more time, is to use someone else's.

CHAPTER SEVEN

FROM THE PIT TO THE PALACE

> For we are God's [own] handiwork (His workman-
> ship) recreated in Christ Jesus, (born anew) that we
> may do those good works which God PREDESTINED
> (planned beforehand) for us [taking paths which He
> prepared ahead of time], that we should walk in
> them [living the good life which He prearranged and
> made ready for us to live].
>
> Ephesians 2:10 (AMP)

There is a remarkable story that has been told about King
Louis the 16th of France. King Louis had been taken from his
throne and imprisoned. His young son, the prince, was taken by
those who dethroned the king. They thought that inasmuch as the
king's son was heir to the throne, they could destroy him morally
if he would never realize the great and grand destiny that life had
bestowed upon him.

They took him to a community far away, and there they
exposed the lad to every filthy and vile thing that life could offer.
They exposed him to rich foods, which would quickly make him a
slave to appetite. They used vile language around him constantly.
They exposed him to lewd and lusting women. They exposed him
to dishonor and distrust. He was surrounded 24 hours a day by

everything that could drag the soul of a man as low as one could slip. For over six months he had this treatment—but not once did the young man buckle under pressure. Finally, after intensive temptation, they questioned him. Why had he not submitted himself to these things? Why has he not partaken? These things would provide pleasure, and satisfy his lusts and desires. The boy said, "I CANNOT DO WHAT YOU ASK; FOR I WAS BORN TO BE KING!"

THE POWER OF DESTINY

The story of Joseph, in the book of Genesis, is an exciting example of the sustaining power of destiny. Joseph was the eleventh of twelve boys in his family. In this large family, which consisted of four wives, and thirteen children, Joseph was highly favored above all the other children by his father.

> **But when his brothers saw that their father loved him more than all his brothers, they hated him and could not speak peaceably to him.**
>
> **Genesis 37:4**

But this story goes on to portray so much more than a boy who was the favorite of his father. The story reveals to us the power of destiny. The Spirit of the Lord delivered destiny into the lap of Joseph in two dreams.

> **Now Joseph had a dream, and he told [it] to his brothers; and they hated him even more. So he said to them, "Please hear this dream which I have**

dreamed: 'There we were, binding sheaves in the field. Then behold, my sheaf arose and also stood upright; and indeed your sheaves stood all around and bowed down to my sheaf!' And his brothers said to him, 'Shall you indeed reign over us? Or shall you indeed have dominion over us?' So they hated him even more for his dreams and for his words. Then he dreamed still another dream and told it to his brothers, and said, 'Look, I have dreamed another dream. And this time, the sun, the moon, and the eleven stars bowed down to me!' So he told [it] to his father and his brothers; and his father rebuked him and said to him, 'What [is] this dream that you have dreamed? Shall your mother and I and your brothers indeed come to bow down to the earth before you?'"

Genesis 37:5-10

Through these dreams God had revealed His plan and destiny for Joseph. A powerful future had been planned for the man with the "coat of many colors." Yet much would happen to this simple man before he would realize his God-given destiny. Because of the dreams, jealousy loomed large in the hearts of Joseph's brothers as they plotted against him.

Now when they saw him afar off, even before he came near them, they conspired against him to kill him. Then they said to one another, "Look, this dreamer is coming! Come therefore, let us now kill him and cast him into some pit; and we shall say,

'Some wild beast has devoured him' We shall see what will become of his dreams!" But Reuben heard [it], and he delivered him out of their hands, and said, "Let us not kill him" And Reuben said to them, "Shed no blood, [but] cast him into this pit which [is] in the wilderness, and do not lay a hand on him"—that he might deliver him out of their hands, and bring him back to his father. So it came to pass, when Joseph had come to his brothers, that they stripped Joseph [of] his tunic, the tunic of [many] colors that [was] on him. Then they took him and cast him into a pit."

Genesis 37:18-24

In a last minute ploy to spare his brother's life Judah said, *"What profit [is there] if we kill our brother and conceal his blood? Come and let us sell him to the Ishmaelites..."* (vs. 26–27).

Potiphar, an Egyptian official, bought Joseph as a slave, but once again Joseph was clothed with favor. Soon he was put in charge of all that was in Potiphar's house. Things had slightly improved from the pit that once held Joseph, but he still was not walking in the manifested destiny God had ordained.

As time passed, Potiphar's wife regarded Joseph. Soon she became the seductress that desired more than Joseph's help around the house. She did her best to entice him into her bed, but Joseph refused to succumb to her temptation. Embarrassed and outraged she cried rape, and soon Joseph once again found himself in the pit, a prison that had no resemblance of the destiny he once dreamed of. (See Genesis 39:6–20)

Even in this state, the favor of the Lord was with Joseph, and soon he was ruling the prison. Destiny, although not yet realized, was still at work bringing Joseph closer to his fate.

When Pharaoh was unable to interpret his troublesome dream, he sought guidance. Joseph was summoned and destiny began to take shape. When Pharaoh told the former prisoner his dream,

Destiny had taken Joseph from the pit to the palace.

Joseph not only interpreted the dream, but he also spoke of how Pharaoh should handle the circumstances and events that were to come. Soon Pharaoh had taken his ring and placed it upon Joseph's finger. Soon Joseph was arrayed in the finest clothes. He was made the head of the whole nation of Egypt. Only Pharaoh held a higher position in all the land. Destiny had taken Joseph from the pit to the palace. In just one day he went from being a common prisoner, to an uncommon leader of the land. He took his place, fulfilled his dreams, and enjoyed his God-given destiny.

> For we are God's [own] handiwork (His workmanship), recreated in Christ Jesus, [born anew] that we may do those good works which God predestined (planned beforehand) for us, (taking paths which He prepared ahead of time) that we should walk in them—living the good life which He prearranged and made ready for us to live.
>
> Ephesians 2:30 AMP

CHAPTER EIGHT

A MIRACLE SETTLES THE ISSUE

Throughout the ages, and in every generation, there is an issue that must be settled. It is an issue of such magnitude that the eternal destiny of every person in that generation depended on its discovery.

The issue: *What is the truth?* What "religion" is right? Whose god is the One True God?

This is exactly the issue the people of Israel had to settle in the Old Testament. Were the people to serve Jehovah, the God of Abraham, Isaac, and Jacob, or were they to serve Baal, alongside his prophets?

We see the dramatic outcome in First Kings 18:

> And it came to pass, when Ahab saw Elijah, that Ahab said unto him, Art thou he that troubleth Israel?
>
> And he answered, I have not troubled Israel; but thou, and thy father's house, in that ye have forsaken the commandments of the Lord, and thou hast followed Baalim.
>
> Now therefore send, and gather to me all Israel unto mount Carmel, and the prophets of Baal four hundred and fifty, and the prophets of the groves four hundred, which eat at Jezebel's table.

So Ahab sent unto all the children of Israel, and gathered the prophets together unto mount Carmel.

And Elijah came unto all the people and said, *How long halt ye between two opinions?* If the Lord be God, follow him: but if Baal, then follow him. And the people answered him not a word.

Then said Elijah unto the people, I, even I only, remain a prophet of the Lord; but Baal's prophets are four hundred and fifty men.

Let them therefore give us two bullocks; and let them choose one bullock for themselves, and cut it in pieces, and lay it on wood, and put no fire under: and I will dress the other bullock, and lay it on wood, and put no fire under:

And call ye on the name of your gods, and I will call on the name of the Lord: *and the God that answereth by fire, let him be God.* And all the people answered and said, It is well spoken.

And Elijah said unto the prophets of Baal, choose you one bullock for yourselves, and dress it first; for ye are many, and call on the name of your gods, but put no fire under.

And they took the bullock which was given them, and they dressed it, and called on the name of Baal from morning even until noon, saying, O Baal, hear us. But there was no voice, nor any that answered. And they leaped upon the altar which was made.

And it came to pass at noon, that Elijah mocked them, and said, Cry aloud: for he is a god; either he is talking, or he is pursuing, or he is in a journey, or peradventure he sleepeth, and must be awakened.

And they cried aloud, and cut themselves after their manner with knives and lancets, till the blood gushed out upon them.

And it came to pass, when midday was past, and they prophesied until the time of the offering of the evening sacrifice, that there was neither voice, nor any to answer, nor any that regarded.

And Elijah said unto all the people, Come near unto me. And all the people came near unto him. And he repaired the altar of the Lord that was broken down.

And Elijah took twelve stones, according to the number of the tribes of the sons of Jacob, unto whom the word of the Lord came, saying, Israel shall be thy name:

And with the stones he built an altar in the name of the Lord: and he made a trench about the altar, as great as would contain two measures of seed.

And he put the wood in order, and cut the bullock in pieces, and laid him on the wood, and said, fill four barrels with water, and pour it on the burnt sacrifice, and on the wood.

And he said, do it the second time. And he said, Do it the third time. And they did it the third time.

And the water ran round about the altar; and he filled the trench also with water.

And it came to pass at the time of the offering of the evening sacrifice, that Elijah the prophet came near, and said, Lord God of Abraham, Isaac, and of Israel, *let it be known this day that thou art God in Israel, and that I am thy servant,* and that I have done all these things at thy word.

Hear me, O Lord, hear me, *that this people may know that thou art the Lord God,* and that thou hast turned their heart back again.

Then the fire of the Lord fell, and consumed the burnt sacrifice, and the wood, and the stones, and the dust, and licked up the water that was in the trench.

And when all the people saw it, they fell on their faces: and they said, The Lord, he is the God; the Lord, he is the God.

1Kings 18:17-39 KJV

Yes, there was an issue at hand that needed to be settled, and a miracle settled the issue!

At the time of Christ, people had long awaited the scriptural fulfillment of the promised Messiah. Jesus came, sent from God, and made some lofty claims.

Could He be the Messiah? Was Jesus the "Son of God" as He was portraying Himself to be?

People had a right to know. The issue had to be settled. The people of that generation and generations to come had a right to know what the truth is.

While John the Baptist was in prison, he heard about the works Jesus was doing and His claim to the Sonship of God. John wanted to know the truth, so he sent his disciples to ask Jesus if He was the promised Messiah.

Jesus did not respond with a theological debate or a doctrinal statement proving who He was. He told the disciples to return and tell John His credentials:

> Go and tell John the things which you hear and see: The blind receive their sight and the lame walk; the lepers are cleansed and the deaf hear; the dead are raised up and the poor have the gospel preached to them.
>
> Matthew 11:4,5

Jesus simply said, *"A miracle settles the issue!"*

At one point, the Jews were ready to stone Jesus because of His claim to be the Son of God. Then Jesus said:

> If I do not do the works of My Father, do not believe Me; *but if I do them,* though you do not believe Me, believe the *works*, that you *may know* and understand that the Father is in Me, and I am in the Father.
>
> John 10:37–38 NASB

Again, Jesus responded with:

> Believe me when I say that I am in the Father and the Father is in me; or at least believe on the evidence of the miracles themselves.
>
> John 14:11 NIV

In Matthew 9:2–7, scribes listening to Jesus demanded proof of His claim to be the Son of God:

> ...they brought to him a man sick of the palsy, lying on a bed: and Jesus seeing their faith said unto the sick of the palsy; Son, be of good cheer; thy sins be forgiven thee.
>
> And, behold, certain of the scribes said within themselves, This man blasphemeth.
>
> And Jesus knowing their thoughts said, Wherefore think ye evil in your hearts?
>
> For whither is easier, to say, Thy sins be forgiven thee; or to say, Arise, and walk?
>
> **But that ye may know that the Son of Man hath power on earth to forgive sins,** (then saith he to the sick of the palsy,) **Arise, take up thy bed, and go unto thine house.**
>
> **And he arose, and departed to his house.**
>
> Matthew 9:2-7 KJV

Jesus offered a miracle as the proof: A miracle settles the issue!

> ...no man can do these miracles that thou doest, except God be with him.
>
> John 3:2 KJV

> ...Jesus of Nazareth, **a man approved of God among you by miracles and wonders and signs,** which God did by him...as ye yourselves also know.
>
> Acts 2:22 KJV

But I have as My witness something greater (weightier, higher, better) than that of John; for the works that the Father has appointed Me to accomplish and finish, the very same works that I *am now doing, are a witness and proof* that the Father has sent Me.

John 5:36 AMP

The issue had to be settled: Was Jesus the Son of God? Time and time again, Jesus offered miracles as proof of who He was. The miracles were His credentials.

A miracle settles the issue!

This issue of what is the truth must be resolved in every generation. In our generation, the question must be answered for the billions of people that cover the earth.

You and I as believers know that truth. We know that Jesus is the Son of God, and we know Him as the only door into the kingdom of God. But what of those who do not know?

> *The miracles were His credentials.*

One cannot merely open a Bible, stand before the more than 800 million Hindus in India, read a passage of scripture, and effectively convince them of the Gospel message. We have our Bible, but they have their Vedas.

We cannot be so naive as to think that if we open our "little black book" filled with scripture verses, we will win the Muslims in Pakistan or Indonesia to Christ as we try to expound on the Word. We have our little black book filled with our scriptures, and the Muslims have their little black book, the Koran, filled with their scriptures.

Take your Bible to Tibet or Japan to convince the Buddhists, and they will quickly counter with their own holy writings, the Tripitaka.

From the Sikhs in Malaysia, to the vast number of Muslims scattered throughout the world, to the witch doctors in Africa, the Bible is nothing more than a "little black book."

Even the highly educated and materialistically engulfed people of Scandinavia, Europe, or the United States have heard the fancy sermons. They have read the Bible, and many have gone to churches. Yet millions in these societies have little regard for the teachings of the Bible. To them, Christianity is just another religion in the world.

Every religious sect, then, can produce as "proof" to their claims their own holy writ. For each of them, *only a miracle will settle the issue.*

Jesus used miracles to draw and convince the masses. Can we use anything less?

> **And a great multitude followed him, because they saw**
> **his miracles which he did on them that were diseased.**
>
> John 6:2 KJV

Only a miracle will convince the masses. Great preaching will not do it. The disciples did not get the job done with great preaching. If great preaching alone could save the world, no one would be lost today.

The Book of Acts is no museum piece. It is a dynamic guidebook on how the Gospel of Jesus, accompanied by the power of the Holy Spirit, penetrates new territory.

How did the Early Church penetrate new territory and the hearts of men?

> And by the hands of the apostles were many signs and wonders wrought among the people....
>
> And believers were **the more added to the Lord, multitudes** both of men and women.
>
> Acts 5:12,14 KJV

> Then Philip went down to the city of Samaria, and preached Christ unto them.
>
> And the people with one accord ***gave heed unto those things which Philip spake, hearing and seeing the miracles which he did.***
>
> Acts 8:5,6 KJV

> ...Peter... came down also to the saints which dwelt at Lydda.
>
> And there he found a certain man named Aeneas, which had kept his bed eight years, and was sick of the palsy.
>
> And Peter said unto him, Aeneas, Jesus Christ maketh thee whole: arise, and make thy bed. And he arose immediately.

And all that dwelt in Lydda and Sharon saw him, and turned to the Lord.

Acts 9:32-35 KJV

And it came to pass in those days, that she [Tabitha] was sick, and died: whom when they had washed, they laid her in an upper chamber....

But Peter put them all forth, and kneeled down, and prayed; and turning him to the body said, Tabitha, arise. And she opened her eyes: and when she saw Peter, she sat up....

And it was known throughout ***all Joppa; and many believed in the Lord.***

Acts 9:37,40-42 KJV

What about the apostle Paul? What kind of a preacher was he? These were his claims:

Through mighty signs and wonders, by the power of the Spirit of God...I have fully preached the gospel of Christ.

Romans 15:19 KJV

My speech and my preaching was not with enticing words of man's wisdom, but in demonstration of the Spirit and of power.

1 Corinthians 2:4 KJV

For our gospel came not unto you in word only, but also in power....

1 Thessalonians 1:5 KJV

Paul claimed miracles as his credentials; the power of the Spirit as his companion.

What was the result of Paul's ministry when he preached with signs and wonders in Antioch?

The next sabbath day came almost the *whole city together to hear* the word of God.

Acts 13:44 KJV

And in Jerusalem, "Then *all* the multitude kept silence, and gave audience to Barnabas and Paul, declaring what miracles and wonders God had wrought..." (Acts 15:12 KJV).

Let's begin by admitting our "programs" do not have a very high success rate.

God still uses signs, wonders, and miracles to reach unbelievers today. Why should He change time-tested, proven ways?

Many have become desensitized to the written and spoken word, but miracles break through barriers once thought impenetrable.

Those who do not know God need to experience Him more than they need to understand Him.

C. Peter Wagner says:

"Across the board, the most effective evangelism in today's world is accompanied by manifestations of supernatural power."

The great missionary statesman T. L. Osborn writes:

It is "this gospel of the kingdom" preached in the power of God, confirmed by signs and wonders and divers miracles, that always produces the greatest evangelistic triumphs in any generation. It is the witness with evidence that convinces. One demonstration is worth a thousand lectures. One miracle is worth a thousand sermons.

Donald A. McGavran, a world-renowned expert in church growth, writes:

"For the last 25 years, I have been studying church growth on the world scene... As I have been reviewing church growth around the world, I have seen that it frequently correlates with great healing campaigns."

In his book, *The Price of God's Miracle-Working Power*, A.A. Allen writes:

"God never called anyone to preach the Gospel without commissioning him to also heal the sick."

Our traditions have blinded us to God-ordained ways to evangelize the lost. Do we need any less demonstration before the godless, atheistic people throughout the world than did the disciples, or Elijah? If the disciples needed this power to give birth to the Church, we need it to preserve the Church and finish the task of the Great Commission.

T. L. Osborn says, "Always preach truth, because truth will always demonstrate. And if you can't demonstrate it, you are not fit to preach it."

It is not the miracles that are significant, but the truth they point to; the reality behind them.

The greatest, most convincing sermons that are ever preached from our crusade platforms come from the lips of the person who only moments earlier was a Hindu or a Muslim. Their message is: "I was blind when I came. Now I see!" Or, "I was paralyzed for years only minutes ago. Now look at me—I can walk! Jesus has healed me!"

In one of our Ugandan crusades, a woman sat at the edge of the crowd, listening. She'd had a large tumor in her stomach for years and had taken four of her goats to four different witch doctors to pay for healing of the tumor. Still it remained.

As she sat at the edge of the field listening to me preach Christ to the multitude, she simply refused to believe the Gospel. But as I prayed for the sick, Jesus instantly melted her tumor, and she came running to the platform, saying, "Believe on Jesus! He is alive! He just took away a large tumor from my stomach!" Now she was a believer. *My words could not convince her, but a miracle settled the issue.*

In our Philippine crusade, the police brought a demoniac, chained hand and foot. As I was preaching, "the power of the Lord was present to heal," and in an instant he was set free. Everyone in the city knew him, and for weeks he testified of Jesus' delivering power, and many believed on the Lord. *A miracle settles the issue.*

In our Nalgonda, India crusade, a tremendous miracle took place outside our hotel room before a night meeting.

Two elderly women came to me for prayer. One of them had been demon possessed for 14 years. As we stood in the courtyard of the hotel, I laid my hands on her head, and the moment I touched her, she fell to the ground in a frenzy. I knelt over her, and the demons began to screech out. Within two minutes, 30 people had come running to see what was happening.

There they were, 30 Hindus watching this American on top of this little Indian woman as she screamed. Then I commanded the evil spirits to come out of her in the name of Jesus.

Suddenly she was set free! As she stood to her feet, her entire countenance had changed, and you could see the peace of God on her.

A Hindu man who had witnessed the deliverance said to me, pointing to the 30 onlookers, "Because of this, *all of us now believe on Jesus.*"

There was no need of a sermon. *A miracle settled the issue.*

We need, and we must have, miracles prevalent in our ministries. Nothing less will satisfy the people of the world, who are crying out for proof of the truth.

In our generation, there is an issue that must be settled. *A miracle settles the issue.*

CHAPTER NINE

WALK ON THE WATER WITH ME

> Now in the fourth watch of the night Jesus went to
> them, walking on the sea. And when the disciples
> saw Him walking on the sea, they were troubled, say-
> ing, "It is a ghost!" And they cried out for fear. But
> immediately Jesus spoke to them, saying, "Be of good
> cheer! It is I; do not be afraid!"
>
> And Peter answered Him and said, "Lord, if it is You,
> command me to come to You on the water!" So He
> said, "COME!" And when Peter had come down out
> of the boat, he walked on the water to go to Jesus.
>
> Matthew 14:25–29

Stop right there! I know the text goes on to say that Peter took
his eyes off the Messiah, looked at the surrounding circumstances,
and begin to sink. I know Jesus rebuked Peter for his lack of faith.
We have all heard, and/or preached, on the failure portion of this
story. It is easy to smugly look at Peter and cast an accusing vote
towards his moment of doubt. Forget about it—the man walked
on the water! Peter acted on ONE word from Jesus and defied the
laws of gravity. With ONE word he took a step into the history
books. Just ONE word allowed this brash disciple, if even for a
moment's time, to be the envy of all onlookers. All it took was just

ONE WORD from Jesus. What could this one word have embodied to cause Peter to do what no mere man had ever done before.

What kind of hidden meaning was interwoven into Jesus' "come"? I took my Strong's Exhaustive Concordance, my Greek Interlinear Lexicon, and looked up the word "come" in the original Greek language. Are you ready for the meaning? The word "come" found here in this text means—COME!

Acting on one word caused the miracle to manifest. Today, if the same scenario would take place in most churches, action would not be the first order on the agenda. Committees would be formed, an open debate would commence, and a vote would be cast. What did Jesus really mean when He said, "Come"? Their final conclusion would be: Let's pray about it, and wait on God for confirmation.

The Word of God is to be acted upon.

We are not to try God's Word. Jesus has already tried and proven it. We simply need to ACT on the Word. Don't ever put a question mark where God has put a period. Many claim to be sound in their doctrine. They are sound, but they are sound asleep.

Too many Christians today are becoming bogged down with the paralysis of analysis. They dissect every little word in the Bible to find its hidden meaning. The Word of God is to be studied and meditated upon, but it is also to be *acted* upon.

We know faith. We talk of faith. Faith is preached from thousands of pulpits across our land. We even know Bible verses about faith in the Greek language. Yet, with all this knowledge of faith, very little faith is ever demonstrated, and it is only in the demonstration of faith that miracles are wrought.

We can know all about the Word of God and be able to quote by heart all the verses about faith, and still be like the people spoken of by the writer of the book of Hebrews, *"...the word which they heard did not profit them, not being mixed with faith in those who heard it"* (Hebrews 4:2).

Hearing the Word of God is not enough. Knowing the Word of God is not enough. It is necessary to ACT on the Word of God. Acting on the Word is faith demonstrated. When faith is demonstrated, then miracles happen.

When Jesus told Peter to come down out of the boat and walk on the water, Peter acted. He did not give heed to reason or yield to surrounding circumstances. He did not consider the consequences of his action. He did not talk of the faith he had; rather, Peter simply ACTED on the word of Jesus. He stepped out of the boat with reckless faith and walked on the water. Peter was a "water walker."

When we first accept Jesus into our lives, everything is fresh and new. The Word of God is alive. We have that same reckless

We do and they recover.

faith that Peter displayed. We read the Bible and believe that what we read is true. We believe that anything can and will happen as we act on the Word of God. We possess a simple child-like faith, one that believes everything we read in the Scriptures.

We read that we can lay hands on the sick, and they will recover. We do and they recover. We read that we can ask for the heathen for our inheritance. We ask, and suddenly the Lord uses us to bring people into the Kingdom of God. If Jesus were to say to us, "Come," we would be gone, walking on the water.

We start out our Christian life daring to believe God for mountains to move. Then a terrible thing begins to happen, we begin to learn. Like Peter, we get out on the water and then learn that we cannot do what we are already doing. We begin to learn that when we act on the Word of God, it does not always work. We begin to learn that our relatives are the toughest ones to win to Christ. We learn that God will sometimes make us sick to teach us a lesson. We learn that we cannot be prosperous because God cannot trust us with money.

Suddenly, the reckless faith that we used to walk in is gone. That reckless faith is replaced with a doubtful question, "What if it does not work?"

Soon we are as full of doubt as we used to be of faith. "What if I lay my hands on someone who is sick and he does not get healed?" "What if I witness to my relatives and they do not want to listen, so they disown me?" "What if I give an offering and God does not bless me?" "What if I step out of the boat and sink?"

I know that in Philippians 3:13–14, the Apostle Paul speaks of forgetting the things which are behind, but I would like for you to reflect back a moment to the time when you first believed. Remember how you jumped out of the boat with reckless faith and walked on the water? Remember how alive the Word of God was in your life? Remember how you believed everything you read, and then acted on that Word?

"What if it does not work?" No, the question is, "WHAT HAPPENS WHEN IT DOES WORK?"

Peter had only ONE word from Jesus. Today we would pull out our pocket promise book and see how many promises the Word gives us for that particular need. One word from God is enough.

For 25 years, I have gone to the nations of the world with only one word from God—GO! I have not waited for confirmation. I did not need another contact. I did not wait until the time seemed to be more conducive. I have gone to more than ninety nations with one word—GO! I have proclaimed the Gospel message to millions. All I have ever had is—GO! The word "go" in the original Greek language means—GO!

"I did my best" is the rallying cry of losers. Winners do not do their best or all they could; they do what it takes. Sometimes that means going beyond yourself and your ability, and into His. *Come on and walk on the water with me!*

One will never start that church until he takes a walk on the water. The lady who possesses the call to the nations will never board that plane until she takes a walk on the water. You will never finance the end-time harvest until you dare to take a little walk on the water. YOU WILL NEVER DEFINE THE FULLNESS OF GOD'S FAVOR UPON YOUR LIFE UNTIL YOU VENTURE INTO THE IMPOSSIBLE AND WALK ON THE WATER WITH HIM.

The Spirit of God is calling us to ACTION. Go and do something. Let God honor both your wisdom and mistakes.

The task ahead is gigantic! We must make strides toward completing the Great Commission. The Body of Christ must be mobilized as soul winning and disciple-making teams to go forth with great fervency. Come and walk on the water with me!

Now when they had gone through Phrygia and the region of Galatia, they were forbidden by the Holy Spirit to preach the word in Asia.

After they had come to Mysia, they tried to go into Bithynia, but the Spirit did not permit them.

So passing by Mysia, they came down to Troas.

And a vision appeared to Paul in the night. A man of Macedonia stood and pleaded with him, saying, "Come over to Macedonia and help us!"

Now after he had seen the vision, immediately we sought to go to Macedonia, concluding that the Lord had called us to preach the gospel to them.

Acts 16:6-10

As we begin to move, divine guidance comes. As we begin to act, divine power is loosed. As we begin our quest for souls on a worldwide scale, the Spirit of God, with His love and Holy Spirit-conviction, will sweep across the continents and usher in the greatest outpouring of the Spirit of God the world has ever known.

When Drs. T.L. and Daisy Osborn ordained me years ago, T.L. spoke a very pertinent word into my life. He told me what an old Methodist man told them when they were young. He said, *"It's not what you know; it's what you do."*

You have been ordained by God to *"go and bring forth much fruit"* (John 15:16).

Come on and walk on the water with me!

Just do it.

CHAPTER TEN

LESSONS FROM THE BOOK OF ACTS

The miracle recorded in Acts 3 caused a great stir in the city. They could not deny it; they could not ignore it. The testimony plagued the religious hierarchy. Their conclusion: threaten Peter and John, and command them to no longer speak in the name of Jesus (Acts 4:17).

After their release, Peter and John turned to the Lord in prayer. They knew the key to the Gospel commission. They knew the keys to successful ministry. Encapsulated in their prayer was the key to the Book of Acts.

> Now, Lord, look on their threats, and grant to Your servants that with all boldness they may speak your WORD, by stretching out Your hand to heal, and that signs and wonders may be done through the NAME of Your holy Servant Jesus. And when they had prayed, the place where they were assembled together was shaken; and they were all filled with the HOLY SPIRIT and spoke the word of God with boldness.
>
> Acts 4:29-31

The three principles practiced in the Book of Acts were:
1. They preached the WORD.
2. They were filled with the SPIRIT.
3. They knew the authority and used the NAME

The WORD convicted of sin and convinced the hearers. The NAME was their credentials and authority.

The HOLY SPIRIT confirmed and produced the signs and wonders. Those are the three keys to the Book of Acts.

T.L. Osborn says, *"Modern theology has entangled the Word in a web of traditional complications. Up-to-date Christendom has limited the Name to a song, an ending of a faithless prayer, or a ceremonial invocation. And streamlined religion has minimized the Spirit to nothing more than a philosophical maxim."*

Too many lifeless churches have turned to "seeker sensitive" methods. Programs have taken the place of power. Events have replaced evidence. The Word has taken a distant place to the world. Many go through the motion, yet seem oblivious to Christ's motive for their lives. Yet, with the great disparity between the example left by the early Church and the modern Church, we know today—there is hope. A return to biblical ways will produce immediate results.

A return to biblical ways will produce immediate results.

Our fathers in the faith preached the Word of God with great boldness. The Holy Spirit worked with them as the anointing caused cities to be shaken. Those faith filled believers wielded an authority by using the Name against demon spirits, diseases, and impossible circumstances. The WORD, the SPIRIT, and the NAME are the three keys to the Book of Acts. These three keys are the keys to world evangelization in our generation.

THE WORD

Peter, Paul, Stephen, and Philip gave the Word a lofty position in their efforts. They spoke the Word of God with great boldness (Acts 4:31). They had been with Christ. They observed the ways in which He had operated. They witnessed the effectiveness of His discipline to operate in ministering the Word. They followed His example and posted these results:

> Then those who gladly received his word were baptized; and that day about three thousand souls were added [to them].
>
> Acts 2:41

> However, many of those who heard the word believed; and the number of the men came to be about five thousand.
>
> Acts 4:4

> Then the word of God spread, and the number of the disciples multiplied greatly in Jerusalem, and a great many of the priests were obedient to the faith.
>
> Acts 6:7

The early Church knew the power of the Word. They knew the results. They had no time for fruitless means of ministry. They gave little place to the dissemination of doctrine. Programs gave way to the proclamation of the Gospel message. Their resolve was unwavering: *"We will give ourselves continually to prayer, and to the MINISTRY OF THE WORD"* (Acts 6:4).

> For I determined not to know anything among you except Jesus Christ and Him crucified. I was with you in weakness, in fear, and in much trembling. And my speech and my preaching [were] not with persuasive words of human wisdom, but in demonstration of the Spirit and of power, that your faith should not be in the wisdom of men but in the power of God.
>
> I Corinthians 2:2-5

Great emphasis is placed on the ministry of the Word through out the Book of Acts. As a result, the Word of God grew and multiplied (Acts 12:24). Paul publicly expounded the Scriptures and many of the Jews were convinced that Jesus was the Christ. The results of His public preaching of the Word: *"On the next Sabbath almost the whole city came together to hear the word of God"* (Acts 13:44).

In nation after nation I have mounted crude wooden platforms. Multitudes gather and I have their attention. The few hours I stand before these people have eternal consequences. Their response and decisions are the most important they will ever make. I have no time for stories, doctrinal dissertations, or programs. It is the WORD. The Holy Spirit takes that Word and convicts of sin and convinces the hearers of the Lordship of Christ.

> Heaven and earth will pass away, but My words will by no means pass away.
>
> Matthew 24:35

You have seen well, for I am ready to perform My word.

Jeremiah 1:12

So shall My word be that goes forth from My mouth; It shall not return to Me void, But it shall accomplish what I please, And it shall prosper [in the thing] for which I sent it.

Isaiah 55:11

He sent His word and healed them, And delivered [them] from their destructions.

Psalms 107:20

For the word of God [is] living and powerful, and sharp-er than any two-edged sword...

Hebrews 4:12

For I am not ashamed of the gospel of Christ, for it is the power of God to salvation for everyone who believes...

Romans 1:16

As the Word is presented there is a natural progression in its affect. First, *"The word of God increased"* (Acts 6:7). Secondly, *"The Word of God grew and multiplied"* (Acts 12:24). Thirdly, *"The Word of God prevailed"* (Acts 19:20).

And they went out and preached everywhere, the Lord
working with [them] and confirming the word through
the accompanying signs. Amen.

Mark 16:20

THE SPIRIT

At the beginning of Jesus' earthly ministry, He stood and proclaimed: *"The Spirit of the LORD [is] upon Me, Because He has
anointed Me To preach the gospel to [the] poor; He has sent Me to
heal the brokenhearted, To proclaim liberty to [the] captives And
recovery of sight to [the] blind, To set at liberty those who are
oppressed..."* (Luke 4:18).

In Acts 10:38, we see that God anointed Jesus with the Holy
Ghost and power, and then He went about healing all who were
oppressed. Heaven ordained the anointing of the Spirit of God as
a prerequisite to ministry.

In what has commonly become known as the Great
Commission, Jesus said to His disciples:

Go ye into all the world, and preach the gospel to
every creature....

And these signs shall follow them that believe....

...they shall lay hands on the sick, and they shall
recover.

Mark 16:15,17–18

Because of this commission that He left to His disciples, Jesus told them to tarry in Jerusalem *"until you are endued with power from on high"* (Luke 24:49).

Jesus knew that the disciples' ministry would have to be carried forth in the power of the Spirit if they were to be effective in their endeavors. Jesus knew that only a ministry that demonstrated the power of God would bring forth the desired fruit.

After all, Jesus needed the manifestation of God's power to be prevalent in His earthly ministry, and His disciples would need nothing less.

THE PATTERN OF THE EARLY CHURCH

First: *"But you shall receive power when the Holy Spirit has come upon you; and you shall be witnesses to Me in Jerusalem, and in all Judea and Samaria, and to the end of the earth."* (Acts 1:8).

Second: *"And they were all filled with the Holy Spirit and began to speak with other tongues, as the Spirit gave them utterance"* (Acts 2:4).

The result: *"And believers were increasingly added to the Lord, multitudes of both men and women"* (Acts 5:14).

The church in the Book of Acts placed a great premium on the power of the Holy Spirit. There are 45 references to the Holy Ghost and 12 to the Spirit, in the Book of Acts. They believed the example of Jesus, and practiced the same.

> Therefore, brethren, seek out from among you seven
> men of [good] reputation, full of the Holy Spirit.
>
> Acts 6:3

And they chose Stephen, a man full of faith and the Holy Spirit...And Stephen, full of faith and power, did great wonders and signs among the people...

Acts 6:5,8

Have you received the Holy Ghost since you believed?

Acts 19:2

Jesus commanded: "Receive the Holy Ghost!"

John 20:22

THE NAME

Tradition blinds mankind to the power behind the Name.

For if by the one man's offense death reigned through the one, much more those who receive abundance of grace and of the gift of righteousness will reign in life through the One, Jesus Christ.

Romans 5:17

From the fall of humanity until the time of the coming of Christ, the human race lived in fear, sin, sickness, poverty, and calamity. Humanity was under the rule of the prince of darkness. But now we have been liberated. Now we can reign in life!

The Word of God tells us:

You shall receive power when the Holy Spirit has come upon you.

Acts 1:8

But even with Scriptures like these, we wonder why that power is not always evident in our lives.

Jesus lives in us. We are the temple of the living God. The zoe (life of God) inhabits our mortal bodies. Romans 8:11 says, *"But if the Spirit of Him who raised Jesus from the dead dwells in you...."* We have the power of God Almighty dwelling on the inside of us! Why, then, is that power seemingly lying dormant in the lives of so many Christians? One author, Charles Trombley, sheds light on that question with this simple statement:

"It takes the authority (exousia) of the exalted Christ, before the power (dunamis) of the indwelling Spirit can be exercised."

A somewhat humorous but really tragic and sad thing I have personally witnessed in some of our overseas campaigns is the

> *We are the temple of the living God.*

way some of the clergy in these foreign countries attempt to deal with demon-possessed people.

I have watched some of these well-meaning but misinformed Christians jump on top of the demon-possessed person while others kicked, punched, and poked at his eyes.

I have also seen them beat the demon-possessed person on the head with their Bibles, trying to bring about their deliverance. They thought by doing these things, the devil would leave.

I have also seen church leaders who were afraid of the devil and what he might do. Although these pastors and evangelists were born-again and Spirit-filled, they knew nothing of the authority they possessed! They did not know how to reign in life through Jesus Christ.

Once, I was ministering in a church near Los Angeles. The first woman who came up in the prayer line told me she needed to be delivered from epilepsy. I laid my hand on her head and she fell to the floor and began to scream. I knelt over her and commanded the spirit to leave in Jesus' Name. Immediately the spirit left, and she was freed and healed from epilepsy. That beautiful Mexican woman lay at the altar and cried, "Gracious Jesus, gracious Jesus, I am free!"

I could relate countless stories of demonic defeat and divine deliverance I have experienced in the last few years. What I want you to know is that it was all done in the Name of Jesus.

Every child of God has the same power over devils and disease. What you need is to discover the authority you have.

While it is true that each born-again, Spirit-filled child of God has the power dwelling on the inside of them, it is true that it takes knowledge of our authority before we can have the power released in our lives.

The early Christians we read about throughout the Book of Acts knew that all of the miracles were done through the Name of Jesus.

The knowledge and use of our authority is what energizes and gives vitality (life) to the power dwelling within each believer. Until you know what you have, you cannot use it!

Authority, in the original Greek text, comes from the word exousia, which means "it is lawful," or "the right to act."

Power comes from the Greek word dunamis, which means "to be able; enabling," or "strength and ability."

Dominion comes from the Hebrew word radah, and it means "to tread down and prevail against," or "to rule and reign."

Although, we have the power of God within us, we need the authority in order to live in the dominion which Christ came to restore back to us. We have been released from the power of darkness, to reign here on earth.

Until you know what you have, you cannot use it!

Jesus gave us the power of attorney to use His Name. He said, in John 15:16: *"...whatever you ask the Father in My name He may give you."*

Again in John 14:13–14 we read:

> **And whatever you ask in My name, that I will do, that the Father may be glorified in the Son. If you ask anything in My name, I will do it.**

This is not prayer. Jesus is giving us the legal right to use His Name to heal the sick, raise the dead, cast out demons, and to meet, as a conqueror, all the forces of darkness.

Jesus gave us the right to use His Name. That is the legal power of attorney.

CHAPTER ELEVEN

I GIVE YOU MY WORLD

My daughter, Breanna, was sound asleep. She was only a few months old at the time I leaned over her crib and had a one-sided conversation with this beautiful new joy in my life.

Welling up from deep within I whispered into her ear, "I give you my world." Behind that simple sentence was the embodiment of all a father's heart could love. I was her daddy. She was my child. I was, and always will be, deeply committed to her. To protect, to guide, to love and provide, my love for my child would have no boundaries.

When I spoke those words "I give you my world" to my little girl, it was the expression of my heart. I would give her all I had at my disposal to make her life better.

When my second daughter Sierra was born, the same commitment flowed from my heart towards her life as well. That is a father's heart.

The Bible tells us: *"If you then, being evil, know how to give good gifts to your children, how much more will your Father who is in heaven give good things to those who ask Him."* Matthew 7:11

The Word of God affords a covenant between the Father in Heaven and those who are His children. One part of the covenant that was born out of a heart of love from God, expresses provision and abundance towards us.

There is an amazing attitude that has conspired against many in the body of Christ today. Scores of well meaning Christians have distanced themselves from the man of God when it concerns their financial well being.

They run to their pastor for counsel when it comes to raising their children. They seek out the man of God's wisdom when their marriage is in need of a revolution. They visit the doctor when sickness appears in the family, but ultimately their confidence rests in God, as they turn to the servants of God for prayer.

When it comes to wisdom, solutions, and counsel concerning financial matters the attitude says: "All the preacher is after is my money." And with that they treat their financial matters as a classified and sealed document that is to be kept away from him.

People tend to trust the man of God with every level of their lives with the exception of their finances. Conventional wisdom sends them to their banker in the hard times. To him they will divulge any and all information. All a banker will ever promise is that if you miss a payment, they will come and take everything you have. Understand this—it is not the job of the bank or lending institution to get you out of debt, it is his job to KEEP YOU IN DEBT.

There are numerous attitudes that will keep us from enjoying all the Father has for us. Our American attitude of debt has caused us to relinquish abundance that has been afforded to us by God. Debt and credit has enslaved most in this land. The interest they offer up to the goddess of debt lends to poverty. But this is the American lifestyle that has been passed down to us.

> Train up a child in the way he should go, and when
> he is old he will not depart from it. The rich rules over
> the poor, and the borrower is servant to the lender.
>
> Proverbs 22:6-7

These verses talk about money. We are instructed to train our children about the dire problems of debt. Yet what example have we portrayed to them? We raise up our children in a house with a thirty year mortgage attached to it. We drive them to school in a car with a five year mortgage on it. They sleep on financed beds and study with financed encyclopedias. Their clothes were bought with credit cards that are washed in a machine that was purchased on a revolving charge account. They are born in a house of debt that they will never see paid. When they turn eighteen we take them to a bank to cosign on their first loan and we launch them into their own ocean of red ink.

The chains of debt can be broken.

Every time your child asks for something—"we can't afford it" is the posted response. If we train and teach our children God's principles of finance, the chains of debt can be broken. Our children can be taught to believe God and practice biblical principles. They need to know money doesn't come from Santa Claus, the Easter bunny, or the tooth fairy.

No one seems to be comfortable talking about money, yet the Bible is full of verses that deal directly with the subject. There are more than 200 verses in the New Testament dealing with money. More than 2,000 verses in the Bible deal with money, while there are only 500 that talk about prayer, and 500 more that address the subject of faith. Sixteen parables in the Word deal with money.

THE NAMES OF GOD

The Names of God express His attributes and give us an understanding of what we can expect.

In Exodus chapter 15 God is revealed to us as "Jehovah-Rapha" the Lord who heals. In Leviticus 20:7–8 God is depicted as "Jehovah-M'Kaddesh," the Lord who sanctifies.

In Judges 6:24 Gideon built an altar and called it "Jehovah-Shalom," or Jehovah our peace. In Jeremiah 23:5–6 "Jehovah-Tsidkenu" means Jehovah our Righteousness. In Psalm 23 He is "Jehovah-Rohi," Jehovah my Shepherd.

In Ezekiel 48:35 He is "Jehovah-Shammah," Jehovah is there. In Exodus 17:15, "Jehovah-Nissi" is my banner. In each of these descriptive Hebrew names of God we are given another revelation of what the Lord is towards His people. Each of these names offer us a clearer understanding of who Jehovah is.

Another significant name comes from Genesis 22. Here the Lord is described as "Jehovah-Jireh," or God will provide. Genesis also ascribes the name "El-Shaddai" to Him. In this name, El-Shaddai, God is seen to be the power or shedder-forth of blessings, the all sufficient and all bountiful One.

The Lord is never referred to as "El Cheapo" or "El Grumpo," yet we act as though we believed that way. When things get tight, we try to back God into a corner and threaten Him with His Word. "Come on tightwad, hand it over. You said You would make my way prosperous, now do it." Often times our attitudes and actions portray us in this very light.

The very nature of God is love and peace. Throughout the Word we read of His hand of healing and prosperity upon those who were His own. Many do not understand the potency of a covenant, nor the transaction side of this powerful force that is available to us.

God leans over and looks upon you with great compassion and uncontainable love. With all the love He has to offer He whispers into your ear, "I give you My world."

Too often we forget who we are. To partake of one's inheritance, proof of identity must be established. We can not partake of our inheritance through an identity crisis. The proof of your right to your inheritance is your identity. You ARE a child of God, never forget that fact.

He says: "I give you my world," not out of duty or obligation. It is out of the love the Father has for His own children. I give all I have to my daughter because I love her. It is not because of merit she has earned or because I owe it—I just love her.

THE DILEMMA OF DEBT

I once asked Pastor John Osteen what he considered to be the greatest key to financial success. He said to me: "Sit on the floor until you can afford a box, then sit on the box until you can afford a chair. Sleep on the floor until you can afford a mat, then sleep on the mat until you can afford a bed." It was quite clear to me what he meant—STAY OUT OF DEBT!

Few things stifle the potency of people and their ministries more than debt. It is this ever soaring debt that keeps people chained to lack—debt keeps you poor and no one listens to a poor man.

> This wisdom I have also seen under the sun, and it seemed great to me:
>
> There was a little city with few men in it; and a great king came against it, besieged it, and built great snares around it.
>
> Now there was found in it a poor wise man, and he by his wisdom delivered the city. Yet no one remembered that same poor man.
>
> Then I said: "Wisdom is better than strength. Nevertheless the poor man's wisdom is despised, and his words are not heard."
>
> Ecclesiastes 9:13-16

Pursuit of the great American dream has buried many under an enormous mountain of debt. Vision to finance the global harvest gives way to the ever mounting stacks of debt. There is no sense in talking about taking the wealth of the sinner when we are financing the world's system with all this debt. Churches and ministries today have buried themselves in so much debt that the focus centers upon the offering times of their services. Hey, what about the world! I like John Osteen's advice—sit on the floor until you can afford a box... Stay out of DEBT!

Stay out of debt!

A NEW ATTITUDE

A tendency in America today seems to strive towards comfortability. People desire to make just enough to keep them in a comfortable lifestyle, they seek to just have enough. This whole thing is not about you, it's about the Kingdom.

Every time an offering is given here in the states that is not matched with one to go towards world missions, we continue to widen the gap between the "haves" and the "have nots."

The Bible tells us in Proverbs 13:22: *"The wealth of the sinner is laid up for the just."* (KJV)

That verse has always been taught in a way that indicates an extraction from the hand of the sinners. A new attitude would say —"let's get them saved and they will populate heaven as they bring their wealth into the Kingdom."

King David possessed a quality and an attitude that forced the blessings of the Lord upon him. In I Chronicles 28 we read a story of how King David depicts his heart concerning the Kingdom.

In verses 2 & 3 we read of David; *"I had it in my heart to build a house of rest for the ark of the covenant of the Lord, and for the footstool of our God, and had made preparations to build it. But God said to me, 'You shall not build a house for My Name's sake, because you have been a man of war and have shed blood.'"*

Reading further into the chapter we see it was David's son, Solomon, who did go on to build the temple David had desired to build. But it was David's attitude that jumps out to me. Even though God told David he could not build the temple, he never told him he could not pay for it!

In I Chronicles 29:2–3 David said:

> Now for the house of my God I have prepared with all my might... Moreover, because I have set my affection on the house of my God, I have given to the house of my God, over and above all that I have prepared for the holy house, my own special treasure of gold and silver...

David's attitude was this—I AM GETTING INVOLVED. He did not sit idly by and see how everything was going to turn out. He determined to get involved. If he could not build it, then he would pay for it. That type of attitude will be blessed. People do nothing because they do not hear God speak. God will not get mad at you for giving too much. If it is good for God, good for people, and good for you—go for it! It

God will not get mad at you for giving too much.

is His will. We do not always have to wait for an audible voice to get involved. The Scriptures also teach— *"as a man purposes in his heart let him give"* 2 Corinthians 9:7. We need BIG KINGDOM thinkers to get this job done. Mohamar Khadafi of Libya pledged one billion dollars to Louis Farakhan, one of the American leaders of the Islamic movement, to further their cause. This kind of action in the Body of Christ will usher in His return. Think BIG enough for God to fit into your thoughts.

CHAPTER TWELVE

POWER TO PROSPER

God has given us a plan for financial success. It is God's will for you to prosper; yet the world seems to be in financial turmoil. Many who are children of the King live in continual fear. Inflation, unemployment, and debt are words and real life experiences that keep many in financial bondage. The economy of many countries today is unstable and their future is uncertain.

Solutions are sought from a wide variety of sources, but seldom from God's Word. We listen to bankers, financial advisors, and loan officers. Great confidence is placed in those who are empowered by your debt and stay in power by keeping you there. Many shun the advice from the source we should seek first—God's Word.

> Jesus the mediator of the New Covenant... see that you do not refuse Him who speaks. For if they did not escape who refused Him who spoke on earth, how much more shall we not escape if we turn away from Him who speaks from heaven, whose voice then shook the earth; but now He has promised saying, "Yet once more, I shake not only the earth, but also heaven." Now this, "yet once more," indicate the removal of those things that are being shaken, as of things that are made, that the things which cannot be shaken may remain. Therefore,

since WE ARE RECEIVING A KINGDOM WHICH
CANNOT BE SHAKEN, let us have grace, by which
we may serve God acceptably with reverence and
godly fear.

Hebrews 12:24-28

We are receiving a Kingdom, which CANNOT be shaken. Although we live in this world and have to work through the world's financial system, we do not have to be subject to it. When

Our financial system is not of this world.

the world's financial system is shaken, the child of God can still stand strong. Our financial system is not of this world. God's financial system cannot be shaken. Neither the rise of inflation, the ever increasing unemployment rate, nor the rise and fall of the world stock markets can ultimately govern our financial stability. WE ARE RECEIVING A KINGDOM, WHICH CANNOT BE SHAKEN.

The King we serve cannot be shaken. The King's Kingdom cannot be shaken. And the King's decree (the Word of God) will never be shaken.

It is God's will that you prosper. Yet just because something is the will of God, does not necessarily mean it will come to pass. If we are to walk in God's prosperity, we must give heed to the King's decree. God's prosperity is governed by biblical principles. His governing laws of financial blessing, His provisional plan, and way to prosperity is plainly laid out—SEEDTIME AND HARVEST.

According to the Bible, the sowing and reaping principle is a God ordained law.

The Bible says, *"If you are willing and obedient, you shall eat the good of the land."* Isaiah 1:19

The Father heart of God desires the best for His children. He desires that you wear the good, drive the good, and have the good of the land. But His word is very plain, if we are to have the "good of the land we must be willing and OBEDIENT. Prosperity demands obedience to the Word of God. You cannot pray prosperity down, it happens God's way. God's way for you to have the good of the land is seedtime and harvest."

Every promise of God is conditional. No promise is unconditional. If you meet the condition to give, then God will fulfill His promise—to give back to you. Prosperity will then be the divine order of the day.

> *Every promise of God is conditional.*

The prosperity doctrine is one of the most misused doctrines in the church today. Many pulpiteers have stripped the power from the Word concerning prosperity, because they have falsely presented seedtime and harvest principles. Too often Bible verses are used as an extraction tool. But still the Word of God calls us to prosperity.

Even though some have abused this message and motives have been wrong, SOWING AND REAPING remains God's financial plan.

And you shall remember the Lord your God, for it is
He who gives you power to get wealth, that He may
establish His covenant...

Deuteronomy 8:18

By no means is it wrong to possess a Rolex watch or Mercedes Benz car, but it is wrong for those things to possess you. God is a jealous God, (Exodus 20:5) and He will prosper us as we keep our affections set on Him. The Word of God states that He wants to give you the desires of your heart, (Psalms 37:4) but the Bible also says He gives you power to get wealth SO HIS COVENANT CAN BE ESTABLISHED ON THIS EARTH! Ultimately this attitude must prevail as our motive in prosperity. God told Abraham: *"I will bless you, so you can be a blessing."* (Genesis 12:2) Prosperity must not be reduced to a tool just to build bigger churches or homes, even though He will bless us with such things. We must prosper to propel the spread of the Gospel message on a global scale. The Gospel is free, but the pipeline to get the Gospel to the world costs money. The Almighty desires for your life to be one of great abundance. His will is for you to eat the good of the land and promote the cause of Christ.

Kenneth Copeland has defined prosperity like this: "True prosperity is the ability to use God's ability and power to meet the needs of mankind, regardless of what those needs may be."

The Bible says, *"You ask and do not receive, because you ask amiss, that you may spend it on your pleasures."* (James 4:3) Keep your heart pure and your affections set on Him, and He will give you the desires of your heart. Impure motives hinder many in their prosperity quest.

Thus says the Lord of hosts: Consider your ways! You have sown much, and bring in little; you eat, but do not have enough; you drink, but you are not filled with drink; you clothe yourselves, but no one is warm; and he who earns wages, earns wages to put into a bag with holes.' Thus says the Lord of hosts: Consider your ways! Go up to the mountains and bring wood and build the temple, that I may take pleasure in it and be glorified,' says the Lord. You looked for much, but indeed it came to little; and when you brought it home, I blew it away. Why?' says the Lord of hosts. Because of My house that is in ruins, while every one of you runs to his own house. Therefore the heavens above you withhold the dew, and the earth withholds its fruit.

Haggai 1:5-10

Too often people are obsessed with building their own empires. Launching out from their parents' domain, the youth of today begin a lifelong scurry to obtain. His Word instructs us to build the kingdom of God. This is the reason some sow much, but reap little. Once again, our motive must be to build the kingdom of God. When our desire for prosperity is to finance the Gospel and win souls, then we will sow much and reap much. It is then that God will give us the desires of our heart. To own the finer things in life is NOT sin. In fact you will only truly enjoy material

> *God's desire is to seek and save the lost.*

things when they become immaterial. God's desire is to seek and save the lost. If you help fulfill the desire of the Father's heart, how much more will He fulfill your heart's desires! The very history of the scriptures tells us that if we will be busy taking care of the Father's business, He will most certainly be busy taking care of ours.

GOD'S WISH

Beloved, I pray that you may prosper in all things and be in health, just as your soul prospers.

III John 2

Let them shout for joy and be glad, who favor my righteous cause; And let them say continually, "Let the Lord be magnified, Who has pleasure in the prosperity of His servant."

Psalms 35:27

Some reduce the Word of God to a religious, powerless pact by their hand-me-down traditions. They teach poverty as a form of holiness. Their commitment to abstain from all, and live a life of poverty, is honored by their followers. Yet we read a different perspective from the Bible:

The thief does not come except to steal, and to kill, and to destroy. I have come that they may have life, and that they may have it more abundantly.

John 10:10

A popular doctrine touted from many pulpits today is one that says: "God has not prospered them, because He cannot trust them with money." While there is an element of truth in the trust aspect, the lack of prosperity cannot be singled out here. Many today are prone to throw the whole premise of prosperity back on God. They say, "I am not prospering because God cannot trust me." Suddenly the burden is back upon the Lord. Now their lack is because "God does not trust me," rather than, "I am not doing my part in the seedtime and harvest principles."

Realize this, MONEY IS THE CHEAPEST THING GOD WILL EVER ENTRUST TO YOU. Think of what The Creator has already entrusted to you: His Name, His Word, and the Great Commission. With such confidence bestowed upon us are we to think now that He cannot trust us with a little bit of money? Yet we are accountable to Him for all.

The reason we have not prospered many times is not because He cannot trust us with money. The reason most do not prosper is because they have not done what the King has decreed. We have not fulfilled our end of the covenant.

> *Keep the King's decree!*

Seedtime and harvest is a God ordained principle. Sowing and reaping is His plan for financial success. It is these principles contained in the law of seedtime and harvest that are absolutely essential to our future as individuals and as the corporate Body of Christ. Keep the King's decree!

THE AMERICAN GOSPEL

I have been privileged to travel to more than ninety nations of the world. America, with all that she stands for, is envied by most in other lands. The vast wealth of this nation and many of her people is more than some in third world countries could ever imagine.

America is a blessed land because she was founded upon Biblical principles. If you are living in a third world nation, don't ever cheapen the Word of God by thinking it will only work in America. Whether you are African or Filipino, heaven's abundance is part of your birthright.

One of the greatest examples I know of in God honoring His Word in the realm of prosperity is that of Dr. Benson Idahosa.

Benson Idahosa was a black African, born and raised in poverty in Benin City, Nigeria. His family was so poor that Benson never owned a pair of shoes until he was eighteen years old.

For several years this dedicated young man pastored a small, poor church in Benin City. No one in his church owned a car. No one owned a motorcycle. He was a poor African, preaching to poor Africans. Nothing of their future seemed to be certain, except more poverty.

While on a trip to America, Dr. Idahosa became aware of the prosperity of many of God's people in the United States. He saw the message of prosperity in the Bible, and the Holy Spirit began to reveal God's will for the Body of Christ. Taking a new-found truth back to Nigeria, Idahosa began to preach prosperity and soon the fruit of this began to blossom.

THE WORD WORKS

The Word works. His great Miracle Centre church has exploded in numbers and in prosperity. Today if you travel to Benin City you will see thousands of prosperous Christians. Members of that great church now drive nice cars and live in fine homes. They are wearing and eating the good of the land.

Idahosa taught those precious Africans that they were created in the image of God. Now they walk tall. He taught them God's will for their lives is prosperity. Today they enjoy the reality of it.

> *Now they walk tall!*

I attended the dedication service of the new 12,000 seat Miracle Centre church. Distinguished guests from all over the world attended. Nearly forty different African kings were there to see the multi-million dollar building. Does prosperity work for anyone? Sure it does. The promise of prosperity has made this man and his ministry a testimony of God's faithfulness to His Word. The Miracle Centre church now sends missionaries out to the world. Prosperity is for you, regardless of place or race!

THROUGH HIS POVERTY

For you know the grace of our Lord Jesus Christ, that though He was rich, yet for your sakes He became poor, THAT YOU THROUGH HIS POVERTY MIGHT BECOME RICH.

II Corinthians 8:9

Prosperity has been provided for us IN REDEMPTION, through the blood of Jesus Christ. One cannot remove prosperity from the redemptive work of Christ, any more than you can remove salvation and healing. Jesus' redemptive work at Calvary has provided salvation, healing, AND PROSPERITY for each of us. It is our birthright as a child of God.

I have a vivid memory of driving into a strange city to preach the Gospel. I can easily recall pulling into the parking lot of a hotel, reclining the seat in my car and struggling to get some sleep so I could preach the next morning. I had no money to actually stay IN the hotel so I stayed in my car in the hotel parking lot.

I remember well the car I used to own. It looked, sounded, and smoked so bad that I used to drive into our church meetings long before anyone else would arrive, and park down the street so no one would see "the embarrassment on wheels."

I remember well those and many other past experiences that help forge character and force our expectancy towards heaven. In my own life I am thankful now for the principles of sowing and reaping that we have learned to live by. Today we are reaping of the harvest and beginning to enjoy His abundant provision.

> I call heaven and earth as witnesses today against you, that I have set before you life and death, blessing and cursing; therefore choose life, that both you and your descendants may live.
>
> Deuteronomy 30:19

It is YOUR choice. You can choose poverty or you can choose prosperity. God has given us the choice. His divine order and plan for prosperity is—SEEDTIME AND HARVEST.

CHAPTER THIRTEEN

FOUNDATION FOR FAITH

The Bible says, "And the prayer of faith shall save the sick, and the Lord shall raise him up ..." (James 5:15 KJV).

The prayer of faith shall save (heal) the sick, but in order to pray the prayer of faith, we must have faith. Faith must have its foundation based upon God's will and God's Word. Building upon anything less will not produce the faith that produces miracles.

> And this is the confidence we have in him, that, if we ask anything according to **his will,** he heareth us.
>
> And if we know that he hear us, whatsoever we ask, we know that we have the petitions that we desired of him.
>
> 1 John 5:14-15 KJV

If we will ask anything according to His will, He has promised to hear and answer. Thus, the key becomes knowing God's will.

God's Word is God's will. Knowing what He has set forth and promised in His Word concerning miracle healing will produce the faith in our hearts, enabling us to pray the prayer of faith.

God's Word is God's will.

GOD'S WILL DECLARED THROUGH THE LIFE OF JESUS

Jesus said, "My meat is *to do the will* of him that sent me" (John 4:34), and, "I have not come to do my own will, but the will of the Father who has sent me" (John 6:38).

What is it that Jesus did while He was here in His earthly ministry? The Bible says that "God anointed Jesus Christ of Nazareth... who went about doing good, and healing all that were oppressed of the devil" (Acts 10:38 KJV).

Throughout the Gospels, chapter after chapter is filled with the testimonies of those whom Jesus healed. With this realization, remember that Jesus came not to do His own will, but the will of the Father.

In Luke 5:12, a man "full of leprosy" came to Jesus seeking God's will concerning healing. He said:

> Lord, if thou wilt, thou canst make me clean.
>
> And he put forth his hand and touched him, saying,
>
> I will: be thou clean. And immediately the leprosy departed from him.
>
> Luke 5:12–13 KJV

Christ's life was lived to declare the will of God. Christ's life demonstrated the will of God in healing all that were brought to Him (Matthew 8:16).

The greatest hindrance to the faith of many seeking healing today is the fact that they are uncertain about God's will in the matter. But the life of Christ should dispel this doubt.

GOD'S WILL DECLARED
THROUGH GOD'S WORD

God's will and God's Word are inseparable, for they are one and the same. It is the Word of God which is the foundation for our faith.

It is our faith, coupled with God's inherent promise to fulfill His Word, that will bring the desired results to our lives and to those to whom we are ministering.

FOUNDATION FOR FAITH

Principle 1: Sickness Does Not Come From God

In order to have faith for miracle healing, you must dispense with any notion you have that says, "God made me sick." What does the Bible say concerning the origin of sickness?

> And, behold, there was a woman which had a spirit of infirmity eighteen years, and was bowed together, and could in no wise lift up herself.
>
> And when Jesus saw her, he called her to him, and said unto her, Woman, thou art loosed from thine infirmity.
>
> And he laid his hand on her; and immediately she was made straight, and glorified God....
>
> The Lord...said...ought not this woman, being a daughter of Abraham, whom Satan hath bound, lo, these eighteen years, be loosed....
>
> Luke 13:11-13,15-16

Whom *God* hath bound? *No!* Whom *Satan* hath bound.

Jesus said in John 10:10, "The thief cometh not, but for to steal, and to kill, and to destroy: I am come that they might have life, and that they might have it more abundantly" (KJV).

Acts 10:38 (KJV) states:

> **God anointed Jesus of Nazareth with the Holy Ghost and with power: who went about doing good, and healing all that were oppressed of the devil....**

You can rest assured that sickness does not come from God. It is a foundation for faith you can build on.

Principle 2: Healing Is Part of God's Covenant

In Exodus 15:26 we find God's contract of healing: "I am the Lord that healeth thee." This covenant is for every child of God. This covenant is for *you!*

In the few words of God's healing covenant, found in this verse, three questions regarding healing are answered.

1. Is God a healer? Answer: Yes. "I am the Lord that healeth *thee.*"

2. Who will God heal? Answer: All. He placed no restrictions and made no exceptions. "I am the Lord that healeth thee."

3. When will God heal? Answer: *Now. "I am* the Lord that healeth thee."

God's covenant of healing includes you. Doctrines of people, contrary to God's Word, are of no consequence to the one whose foundation of faith is built upon His Word. You can try to exclude yourself or even others, but God excludes no one. The traditions of man never work the purposes of God.

And you shall serve the Lord your God, and he shall bless thy bread, and thy water; and I will take sickness away from the midst of thee.

Exodus 23:25 KJV

There is no waiting. There is no grace period. He said, *"I am the Lord that heals you."* God's covenant is a foundation for faith you can build on.

Principle 3: Healing Was Included in Christ's Atonement

Most have no problem including, as part of Christ's atonement, the forgiveness of sins. When it comes to the issue of healing, however, healing is often looked at with skepticism. But God's Word is clear, and it does not omit healing from Christ's substitutionary act.

Surely he has borne our griefs, and carried our sorrows: yet we did esteem him stricken, smitten of God, and afflicted.

But he was wounded for our transgressions, he was bruised for our iniquities: the chastisement of our peace was upon him; and with his stripes we are healed.

Isaiah 53:4–5 KJV

A more literal translation reads:

Certainly he has suffered our pains and carried our diseases… and with his stripes we are healed.

The psalmist David declares of Christ's redemptive work, "Who forgiveth all thine iniquities; who healeth all thy diseases" (Psalm 103:3 KJV).

Noting that Jesus had just healed all that were sick, Matthew echoes the prophet Isaiah and writes:

> **That it might be fulfilled which was spoken by Esaias the prophet, saying. Himself took our infirmities, and bare our sicknesses.**
>
> **Matthew 8:17 KJV**

Do not count yourself or anyone you may be ministering to "out." The "our" and the "you" included in these texts includes you. Peter says:

> **Who his own self bare our sins in his own body on the tree, that we, being dead to sins, should live unto righteousness: by whose stripes ye were healed.**
>
> **1Peter 2:24 KJV**

The apostle Paul, speaking of Christ's redemptive work, writes to the Galatians, "Christ has redeemed us from the curse of the law..." (Galatians 3:13).

What was included as part of the curse we have been redeemed from? *"Every sickness"* (Deuteronomy 28:60,61).

Never can physical healing be scripturally separated from salvation: "Jesus, for he shall save his people..." (Matthew 1:21). "For God sent not his Son into the world to condemn the world; but that the world through him might be *saved"* (John 3:17 KJV). The term "saved" always included the benefits of salvation.

The words "save," found in Luke 9:56, First Corinthians 1:21, and James 5:15, and "saved," from Mark 16:16, Luke 7:50, John 3:17, Acts 4:12, Romans 10:9, and Ephesians 2:8, are all translated from the Greek word *sozo,* which means "to save, deliver, protect, heal, preserve, be whole, and to make whole."

The words "healed" in Mark 5:23, Luke 8:36, and Acts 14:9, and "whole" in Matthew 9:21,22, Mark 6:56, Mark 10:52, Luke 17:19, and Acts 4:9 are also translated from the same Greek word *sozo,* which means the same here as it does in the scriptures above.

Spiritual and physical healing are included in everyones salvation. You cannot separate the Savior from the Healer. Neither can you separate healing from salvation.

Christ's atoning, substitutionary act on the cross has made forgiveness and healing available to you. Christ's atonement is a foundation for faith you can build on.

Principle 4: Healing Was Part of Jesus Ministry

A careful look at the Gospels shows us what an integral part miracles and healing had in the ministry of Jesus.

> When the even was come, they brought unto him many that were possessed with devils; and he cast out the spirits with his word, and healed all that were sick.
>
> Matthew 8:16 KJV

> ...and great multitudes followed him, and he *healed them all.*
>
> Matthew 12:15 KJV

> And the whole multitude sought to touch him: for there went virtue out of him, and healed them all.
>
> Luke 6:19 KJV

Now when the sun was setting, all they that had any
sick with divers diseases brought them unto him
and he laid his hands on every one of them, *and
healed them.*

Luke 4:40 KJV

Healing was definitely a large part of Christ's ministry. The
Bible tells us that "Jesus Christ [is] the same yesterday, and *today,*
and for ever" (Hebrews 13:8 KJV). And that is a foundation for
faith you can build on.

Principle 5: Healing Was Part of Christ's Commission

In what has commonly become known as the Great
Commission, Jesus said to His disciples:

Go ye into all the world, and preach the gospel to
every creature....

And these signs shall follow them that believe....

...they shall lay hands on the sick, and they shall recover.

Mark 16:15,17,18 KJV

Because of this commission that He left to His disciples, Jesus
told them to tarry in Jerusalem "until you are endued with power
from on high" (Luke 24:49).

Jesus knew that the disciples ministry would have to be carried
forth in the power of the Spirit if they were to be effective in their
endeavors. Jesus knew that only a ministry that demonstrated the
power of God would bring forth the desired fruit.

After all, Jesus needed the manifestation of Gods power to be prevalent in His earthly ministry, and His disciples would need nothing less.

Healing is part of the Gospel. Jesus said, "Preach the Gospel in all the world" and "to every creature." If it was not His will for "every creature" to receive the blessings and benefits of healing, He would not have commissioned us to such a task.

The fact that Jesus commissioned His servants to bring the Gospel, which included healing, to *every creature* adds additional proof of His will. Christ's commission is a foundation for faith you can build on.

Principle 6: Healing Was Part of the Early Church's Example

The Book of Acts has been left to us as a blueprint and a design of Gods plan for His Church. The Early Church is our example for the operation of our ministries.

The Bible says that "...many wonders and signs were done through the apostles" (Acts 2:43). Miracles and healings were one of the main ingredients found in the Early Church throughout the Book of Acts.

One day as Peter and John were going to the Temple for prayer, they came across a crippled man who was sitting at the Gate Beautiful, begging. When this beggar asked Peter and John for alms, he was in store for much more than he was bargaining for!

Peter said to him, "In the name of Jesus Christ of Nazareth rise up and walk" (Acts 3:6 KJV); and when Peter took him by the right hand and lifted him up, "immediately his feet and ancle [ankle] bones received strength" (verse 7). And he went into the Temple walking, and leaping, and praising God (verse 8).

The miracle testimony spread throughout the city of Jerusalem and stirred the hearts of people. Even the scribes, Pharisees, and Sadducees could do nothing to persuade the people of their conviction that this was not from God. They conferred among themselves and finally said:

> What shall we do to these men? For that indeed a notable miracle hath been done by them is manifest to all them that dwell in Jerusalem; and we cannot deny it.
>
> Acts 3:16 KJV

The ministries we read about in the Book of Acts were laced with miracles. It was God's way, and it was God's will.

Miracles were prevalent in the apostles' ministries:

> Insomuch that they brought forth the sick into the streets, and laid them on beds and couches, that at the least the shadow of Peter passing by might over-shadow some of them.
>
> ...and they were healed every one.
>
> Acts 5:15–16

> Stephen, full of faith and power did great wonders and miracles among the people.
>
> Acts 6:8

> And the people with one accord gave heed unto those things which Philip spake, hearing and seeing the miracles which he did.
>
> Acts 8:6

And there sat a certain man at Lystra, impotent in his feet... who had never walked:

The same heard Paul speak: who stedfastly beholding him, and perceiving that he had faith to be healed,

Said with a loud voice, Stand upright on thy feet. And he leaped and walked.

Acts 14:8-10

We must endeavor to follow the pattern and example of the Early Church in everything we do. Miracles had a prominent place in their example.

The example of the Early Church and their emphasis on miracles is a foundation for faith we can build on.

God is not a man, that he should lie; neither the son of man, that he should repent, hath he said and shall he not do it? or hath he spoken, and shall he not make it good?

Numbers 23:19 KJV

There hath not failed one word of all his good promise....

1 Kings 8:56 KJV

Forever, O Lord, thy word is settled in heaven.

Psalm 119:89 KJV

...I will hasten my word to perform it.

Jeremiah 1:12

For the word of God is quick, and powerful, and sharper than any two edged sword....

Hebrews 4:12

All scripture is given by inspiration of God...

2 Timothy 3:16

The word of the Lord endureth for ever.

1 Peter 1:25

The grass withereth, the flowers fadeth: but the word of our God shall stand for ever.

Isaiah 40:8

So shall my word be that goeth forth out of my mouth: it shall not return unto me void, but it shall accomplish that which I please, and it shall prosper in the thing whereto I sent it.

Isaiah 55:11

These are promises you can count on!

CHAPTER FOURTEEN

STONE MOVERS/WORLD SHAKERS

You must harbor a passion to champion a cause.

The motivating passion that governs my life is—souls! It is this

> ## *You must harbor a passion to champion a cause.*

passion that dictates the focus of my thoughts and my energies.

My message is not one-sided; rather, it comes from a singleness of heart.

The great revival writer Leonard Ravenhill states in *Why Revival Tarries:*

We have many organizers, but few agonizers; many players and payers, few prayers; many singers, few clingers; lots of pastors, few wrestlers; many interferers, few intercessors, many writers, but few fighters. Failing here, we fail everywhere. The two prerequisites to successful Christian living are *vision and passion!* [author's italics]

Almost one million people die each week in the world without the knowledge of Christ. Is that nothing to you? Have you a pain in your heart for perishing people?

A quenchless zeal for the lost and a passion for souls is what has driven me to seek out the most effective methods of worldwide soulwinning. Miracle evangelism, initiated by Jesus, carried out by the Early Church, and proven in generations past and in the present is the most effective method of fulfilling the Great Commission.

The cause I march for—to fulfill the Great Commission and to bring the world to Christ. The passion I embrace—a passion for souls and a heartfelt passion to be used as an instrument of God's power to make my soulwinning efforts effective.

By the year 2000, Islam will have more than one billion followers. By the year 2000, India will host more than one billion inhabitants. (Presently, the Christian population of India is less than one percent.)

It is time to move into the arena of world evangelization actively! Praying for lost sinners to see the light was not the Master's approach to evangelism. This is not what He instructed us to do.

Do you realize that Jesus does not pray for lost sinners or for the harvest? He said, "I do not pray for the world ..." (John 17:9).

Regarding the role of prayer in world evangelism, we find it was limited in scripture to Jesus' instruction in Matthew 9:38, "Pray the Lord of the harvest to send out laborers into His harvest."

How often has the Spirit of the Lord prodded us to be the answer to that prayer?

How often men of God hide behind their position of pastor, evangelist, or teacher, defining that role as "perfecter of the saints," equipping the Church for the work of the ministry so they can enter into the soulwinning harvest. Like pastor, like people. People follow an example, but only listen to words.

The responsibility for demonstrating God's miracle power to the unbeliever rests upon every believer.

Do you not say, "Four months more and then the harvest"? I tell you, open your eyes and look at the fields! They are ripe for harvest.

"Even now the reaper draws his wages, even now he harvests the crop for eternal life, so that the sower and the reaper may be glad together."

John 4:35,36 NIV

Look! The wages you failed to pay the workmen who mowed your fields are crying out against you. The cries of the harvesters have reached the ears of the Lord Almighty.

You have lived on earth in luxury and self-indulgence.

James 5:4,5 NIV

A life of significance. A ministry of fruitfulness. A passion with a directive of winning lost multitudes. Can anything less than this satisfy you?

A passion for souls will lead you into a search for the most effective ways to evangelize. This journey of searching for these methods of fruitful evangelism will lead you to ask one question for your life: What must I do that I might work the works of God?

STONE MOVERS/WORLD SHAKERS

Faith does not weigh alternatives; faith acts on assurances. Faith is not believing in spite of *circumstances;* faith is believing in spite of *consequences*.

Many today indignantly proclaim, "The day of miracles is past." Know this: There never was "a day of miracles." There *is* a God of miracles!

T.L. Osborn says, "The love of the miraculous is not a mark of ignorance, but rather reveals man's intense desire to reach the unseen God."

It is not wrong to desire the miraculous. The God we serve is a miracle-working God.

But in order for the miracles of God to be produced, there must be faith, which is dependent upon hearing the Word of God (see Hebrews 11:6 and Romans 10:17). If we are to see the miracles we read about in the New Testament, we must proclaim God's Word today, the same as it was preached in those days.

> **And they [the disciples] went forth, and preached every where, the Lord working with them, and confirming the word with signs following.**
>
> **Mark 16:20 KJV**

A ministry not producing miracles may very well be a ministry not preaching the Word of God. The Bible says that the Lord worked with Jesus' followers *"confirming the word* with signs following." God cannot confirm what has not been proclaimed.

> **And this gospel of the kingdom shall be preached in all the world for a witness to all nations; and then shall the end come.**
>
> **Matthew 24:14 KJV**

As we have previously mentioned, the word "witness" that is used here means "with evidence or proof." Jesus said that the Gospel will be preached as a witness—in other words, *with evidence, in proof.* The Gospel will be preached "with signs [evidence, proof] following."

You may say to yourself, "I preach the Gospel. I hear the Word of God. I have read the Word, and I believe what it says."

Yet with this testimony, you will clamor and echo Gideon, saying:

> ...Where are all His miracles which our fathers told
> us about....?
>
> Judges 6:13

What must you do to work the works of God? The answer is found in this text:

> And many of the Jews had joined the women around Martha and Mary, to comfort them concerning their brother.
>
> Then Martha, as soon as she heard that Jesus was coming, went and met Him, but Mary was sitting in the house.
>
> Then Martha said to Jesus, "Lord if You had been here, my brother would not have died..."
>
> And He said, "Where have you laid him?" They said to Him, "Lord, come and see."
>
> Jesus wept.
>
> Then the Jews said, "See how He loved him!"

And some of them said, "Could not this Man, who opened the eyes of the blind, also have kept this man from dying?"

Then Jesus, again groaning in Himself, came to the tomb. It was a cave, and a stone lay against it.

Jesus said, "Take away the stone." Martha, the sister of him who was dead, said to Him, "Lord by this time there is a stench, for he has been dead four days."

Jesus said to her, "Did I not say to you that if you would believe you would see the glory of God?"'

Then they took away the stone from the place where the dead man was lying....

And he who had died came out....

John 11:19-21,34-41,44

Realize this: Jesus could have moved the stone. He could have summoned 10,000 angels to carry the stone away. He could have shaken the earth, causing the stone to roll away.

Even though Jesus could have moved the stone, He didn't. Instead, He said, "Take away the stone."

Where is your miracle? *It's in the cave, behind the stone!*

How do you get your miracle? *Move the stone!*

How do you move the stone to release the God of miracles and the miracles of God? *Do what the Word of God says to do!*

The miracle of Lazarus being raised from the dead was in the cave. The miracle could not take place until faith was demonstrated.

Without faith, there is no miracle. Only in a demonstration of faith are miracles wrought. Acting on or doing the Word is faith demonstrated.

EVANGELIST
MIKE FRANCEN

Mike Francen has travelled to over 93 countries
around the world and has seen the Gospel of Jesus
transform the lives of millions of people.

FRANCEN WORLD OUTREACH
HEADQUARTERS

Mike and Jamie Francen in front of their 35,000 square foot world headquarters office complex.

Masses & Miracles mark the first 25 years of FWO

HONDURAS
EL PROGRESO

GUATEMALA

EL SALVADOR

The people were hungry for God in:
El Progreso - Honduras, Guatemala, & El Salvador.

The Stadiums & Fields overflowed with a Harvest of Souls.

BRAZIL

HONDURAS
SAN PEDRO SULA

PARAGUAY

The Gospel was heard by the masses in:
Brazil, San Pedro Sula - Honduras, & Paraguay.

Manila - Philippines, Sattenapalle - India, & El Salvador will never be the same.

PHILIPPINES
MANILA

INDIA
SATTENAPALLE

EL SALVADOR

No matter what language is spoken, God's Word proves itself with Signs & Wonders!

GUINEA

BOLIVIA

INDIA
KAKINADA

Guinea, Bolivia, & Kakinada - India
were seeded with the Gospel of Jesus Christ.

A Sea of People creating a Tidal Wave of Praise!

WEST AFRICA
BENIN

LIBERIA
BUSHROD ISLE

LIBERIA
MONROVIA

COSTA RICA

In 93 Nations Signs and Wonders Convince the Multitudes of God's Power and Love for Them!

CAMEROON

SINGAPORE
RMI CRUSADE

URUGUAY

The response of the crowds is evidence that, "A Miracle Settles the Issue."

Captives were set free!
The lame walked!
Heaven rejoiced!

INDIA
NAGPUR

INDIA
HYDERABAD

THAILAND

INDIA
MADHYA PRADESH

MADAGASCAR

More than 11,000,000 Souls have been Harvested for the Kingdom of God over the past 25 years!

PERU
IQUITOS

TOGO
WEST AFRICA

TANZANIA
MWANZA

When ears are opened, hearts are soon to follow.

Changing the eternal course of a Nation; thousands at a time!

HONDURAS
LA CEIBA

INDIA
VIJAYAWADA

PERU
AREQUIPA

The joy of the Lord can truly be seen in the dance of the one who was lame.

When the Power of God falls, the hands of the people rise in praise.

INDIA
INDORE

NICARAGUA
MANAGUA

CHILE
ARICA

The heart of the forgiven overflows with praise!

Franeens & Osborns

Join Hands

Fire Conference ~ Hyderabad, India

Fire Conference ~ Manila, Philippines

Bibles and books distributed in India

SUPPLING SEED TO THE SOWER 2 COR 9:10
50,000 BIBLES 110,000 BOOKS
SEEDING INDIA'S FUTURE...TODAY.

T. L. Osborn has been a mentor, hero, inspiration, and close friend since 1984. I consider some of the joint campaigns we have done together to be among the highlights of our first 25 years of global evangelism.

Taking the message of God's Love around the world in the name of Jesus!

Fraurens & Osborns

Join Hands

Good News & Healing Festival – India

Quest for Souls Campaign – Manila, Philippines

Philippines India Honduras

Thousands of lives were brought out of the darkness and into the Light of God's Grace!

THROUGH THE YEARS

Top: 1985 - First India Crusade.
Since then we have taken 28 trips
to India and have had more than
40 crusades in this great land.

Bottom: In Suriname scores of people
flooded the City Square in 2000.

Mike has been blessed with many honors over the years.

In 1987 Mike was ordained by T. L. & Daisy Osborn

Mike was awarded an honorary Doctorate of Divinity by Charles H. Mason University.

In 1999 Mike was awarded a Doctorate of Philosophy in Missionary Evangelism by Life Christian University.

Miracles & Multitudes have marked the first
25 years of Francen World Outreach.

THROUGH THE YEARS

20 Year Anniversary Crusade
San Salvador, El Salvador – February 2005

Top: A gift for a local orphanage.

Bottom: Mike and Jamie celebrate with their children at the crusade.

FWO 20 Year Anniversary Crusade

The largest gathering of believers in the History of El Salvador, saw the Power of God poured out on all flesh, from the President of their country to the smallest child!

Mike prays for President Saza

Making Headlines
and
Writing History

La Haya, el único camino

☞82 y

Oran por un gobierno con sabiduría para Honduras

INSUFICIENTE resultó ayer el estadio "Morazán" para las miles de personas que llegaron a escuchar el mensaje esperanzador que trajeron los predicadores estadounidenses Mike France y T. L. Osborn en su cruzada "Invasión 2000", quienes oraron para que Honduras se recupere de las heridas por los desastres naturales y para que el presidente Carlos Flores, al centro de espalda, gobierne el país con sabiduría.

Según cálculo...
Fraternidad de ...
res de Arica, el ... in
lista norteame...red
Mike Francen ...
a cerca de 30 ...ing
sonas en los cl...ual
que duró su Cr...her
Milagros, en la ... of
da ubicada fre...ther
Piscina Olín... ...es.
(PAGINA ...ers)

Acto se efectuará esta tarde en 21 de Mayo con P...

Concentración de Lavín en A...
Página A 7

TE GOVT.

headquarters on Broad Street, beginning at
cont'd on page 4

Francen crusade works wonders

Visiting American Evangelist Mike Francen and team early this week commenced a six-day (February 25-March 1) miracle healing crusade at the NPA Sports Pitch on Bushrod Island. Many amazing events have been taking place. Thousands of Christians and curious onlookers have been touched in a mighty way by this powerful man of God.

Through the Years

Making Headlines and Writing History

SPORTS TRACK MARCH 25-31 1995

JESUS CHRIST IS THE SAME YESTERDAY, TODAY, AND FOREVER.........HEB. 13:8

MIRACLE, HEALING AND SALVATION CRUSADE WITH EVANGELIST

MIKE FRANCEN

Evangelist Francen leading thousand into a time of decision for Jesus-(Salvation).

Evangelist francen with several clutches in hand of those who had been healed

Mike Francen

Un evangelista sana

'TIME FOR PEACE'

"This is the time that God has appointed for the war in Liberia to stop for peace to be restored once more," said Evangelist Mike cont'd on page 10

Evangelist Francen holds up crutches of several disabled persons healed by the power of God (See more pictures on center spread)

Making Headlines and Writing History

CRUZADA DE MILAGROS CONMOCIONO IQUITOS

Tú que escucha al pastor milagrero: Vilma Plata hubiera dado un ojo de la cara por semejante convocatoria.

MILAGROS PARA OLVIDAR LA CRISIS

Llenaron la Plaza Villarroel durante tres noches. Mike Francen, un pastor norteamericano que sólo habla inglés, logró seducir a una multitud de fieles evangelistas que concurrieron a la ceremonia con la esperanza de curar sus males, no solo espirituales. Algunos afirman que lo lograron.

De foto toont een deel van de ruim 7000 mensen, waarvan enkele in rolstoel zaten, die gisteren de evangelisatie-wonderen campagne van het Osaf-Aankutjksdotsplats bijwoonden. Zij mochten getuige zijn van de vele wonderen of ontvingen ze zelf een. Foto: Johan de Randamie

Evangelisatiecampagne Francen:
Gods Geest liet velen genezing ontvangen

door Roy Bruce

Een goed aantal mensen heeft gisteren, door het geloof in God, genezing mogen ontvangen tijdens de eerste dag van de evangelisatiecampagne van Mike Francen. Wonderbaarlijk was vooral het feit dat een jongen die maakt kon lopen, genezing door Jezus Christus, aetiolog en enkele minuten later uit blijdschap op het podium rende. Ruim 7000 mensen mochten getuige zijn van dit wonder.

Evangelist Mike Francen is een man met een roeping van God. Zijn verlangen is om miljoenen mensen te bereiken met het evangelie. Dit doel verwezenlijkt Francen door het opzetten van grote evangelisatie/wonderasan pagnes. Mike, die afgelopen donderdag in Suriname arriveerde en gisteren de eerste campagne hield, heeft al meer dan 50 landen over de gehele wereld bezocht. De campagne in Suriname staat onder de thema: "Jezus Christus is kaban en gisteren deszilfde en tot in eeuwigheid".

hield", Het groot aantal bezoekers gisteren op het Oosthaven-lijksweiplats kenmerkt niet alleen uit gelovigen, maar ook uit belangstellenden. Een deel van hen kon hun hart opmaken, om ook een aanraking van de Heilige Geest te krijgen en Christus in zijn leven aan te nemen.

Velen waren vooral onder de indruk van de wijze waarop Francen, geleid door de Heilige Geest, op een vondige en ook begrijpelijke wijze het Woord van God aan de mensen overbracht. Hij riep vooral de mensen die voor genezing aanwezig waren op om niet op een gebed van hen te wachten, maar wel te wachten, totdat lm. Francen gaf tijdens de campagne als voorbeeld, dat toen hij kort voor zijn ac-

kont in een ander land en wel voor de tweede maal, hij door journalisten gevraagd werd wat de mensen van hem mochten verwachten. Volgens Francen moesten mensen niets van hem verwachten maar juist van God.

WERKING
De werking van de Heilige Geest gistravond was duidelijk, want even later betraden de mensen die genezing hadden ontvangen het podium om van het wonder dat de zijwing jaar lang niet kon lopen, dit gisteren wel, terwijl twee meisjes van 11 en 15 jaar weer konden praten. Verder ontvingen ook een man die al eens genezing aan zijn rug. Hij was natuurlijk hij een aanrij-

ding betrokken geweest en moest zich sinds toen met een kruk voortbewegen. Vanmorgen hield Francen een conferentie in de Congreshal. Hij riep de mensen gisteren op om vandaag met vriend, familielid of kennis naar te mensen.

Millenniumtop
Verenigde Naties afgesloten

De Millenniumtop van de Verenigde Naties in New York is afgesloten met het samensen van een Millennium-verklaring. Hierin zijn de belangrijkste doelen voor de Verenigde Naties in de 21e eeuw vastgelegd. In de verklaring staat onder meer dat de strijd moet worden aangegaan tegen armoede en ziektes als aids.

Side by side
for the
Glory of God!

THROUGH THE YEARS

TWO has seeded millions of Mike's books into the Nations of the World.

Millions have viewed the award winning Docu-Miracle Films around the world.

INVASION 2000
6000 DOCU-MIRACLE FILMS SEEDED

ONE MILLION BOOKS
SEEDING HONDURAS

His words are still true…

"The Harvest is Ripe."

West Africa Crusade

A Miracle Settles the Issue!

SIGNS AND WONDERS

In the aftermath of a Miracle, lay the crutches of the past and a hope for the future!

SIGNS AND WONDERS

And these signs will follow those who believe in My Name...

Train Track To Glory Tour
INDIA

Over 800
Preachers
on Board!

Traveling by train
for 5 days in 17 cars
totaling over 1/3 mile long.

Train Track To Glory Tour
INDIA

Distributed:
130,000 Books,
50,000 Bibles, &
500,000 Tracts

Gospel train draws multitudes

EXPRESS NEWS SERVICE

Visakhapatnam, Jan 15: About 600 preachers who arrived in a special gospel train here on January 13, preached the word of God to people.

The preachers, after arrival here, went to Gurajada Kalakshetram singing hymns in praise of God, where they addressed a huge congregation of people. The main sermon was given by Mike Francen who later prayed for people with sickness. Those healed by his prayers gave their testimony, sharing the dais with him. It was followed by cultural programmes.

The meeting here was organised by Director General of Police (retired) K Rushya Rao who is also the chief patron of the State Gospel Train. The train left for Vizianagaram.

Built 10 Well of Life Churches!

TRAIN TRACK TO GLORY TOUR
THAILAND

Renting an entire Train we impacted an entire nation!

10,000 Families were fed

10 Well of Life Churches

100,000 Books were given

5 Mobile Evangelism Units given

Distributed 500,000 tracts.
Treated hundreds medically.
Provided 3,500 blankets to the poor.

TRAIN TRACK TO GLORY TOUR
THAILAND

A Historic event in six days & eight cities!

PITSANULOKE

PHRAI

PIJIT

Over 400 believers on board

Thousands gave their lives to Christ in this Mystical Land.

The Amazon
RIVER OF LIFE TOUR

Five Boats Invaded the Amazon River

Our team of 453

Well of Life

Well of Life

Navigating the Mighty Amazon

The towns were filled with joy

Well of Life

A Gospel Invasion of South America for the Kingdom of God!

The Amazon
RIVER OF LIFE TOUR

A Nation was Harvested

NAUTA

TAMSHIYACU

REQUENA

ESPERANZA

IQUITOS

We conducted crusades along the way,
sowed a well drilling machine, and much more!

The Amazon
RIVER OF LIFE TOUR

A Region was Seeded

100,000 Books

M.E.U.

Book Packets Assembled

5 River M.E.U.s

We completed 10 "Well of Life" projects and treated 1,134 people on the Medical Boat!

Writing History
Making Headlines
Seeding a Nation

Three Airplanes with more than 400 U.S. believers were greeted by thousands at the Airport Reception!

A Lasting Impression was left on this Nation.

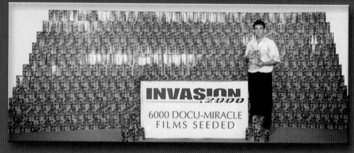

One <u>MILLION</u> books given, 6,000 Docu-Miracle films donated, and a Well of Life church was built for this great land.

A Gospel Invasion does not stop at the Capital Steps

Over 12,000 attended the Fire Conference

Headlines were made as Mike and T. L. prayed for the President of Honduras.

Over 130,000 saw
the Power of God
during the crusade.

The deaf could hear for the first time,
the lame could walk on legs never before used,
and the sick were made whole for the Glory of God.

THE VISION
TRAIN & EQUIP NATIVE MINISTERS

Tons of Bibles & Gospel Literature

INDIA

PHILIPPINES

INDIA

EL SALVADOR

Seeding nations with the Word of God, expecting a harvest of Signs & Wonders!

THE VISION
TRAIN & EQUIP
NATIVE MINISTERS

Believers are
Learning today &
Leading tomorrow!

BRAZIL

PARAGUAY

HONDURAS

Over One Million books
distributed in Honduras alone!

THE VISION
TRAIN & EQUIP
NATIVE MINISTERS

The Conferences are sparking a passion for God!

PERU

LIBERIA

INDIA

Over 8,000 people attended the Liberia Conference!

Well of Life Projects Around the World

To Date We Have Completed 567 projects, Our Goal: 1,000

The Well of Life Projects are an effective church planting endeavor where we share the love of God in a very tangible way. We target remote villages that do not have access to fresh drinking water, and go into these villages to drill a well and install a pump. We also construct a church and hold a special dedication service to offer the natural water and the true "Living Water" of Jesus Christ. These projects are proving to be one of the greatest church planting and soul winning methods of our day.

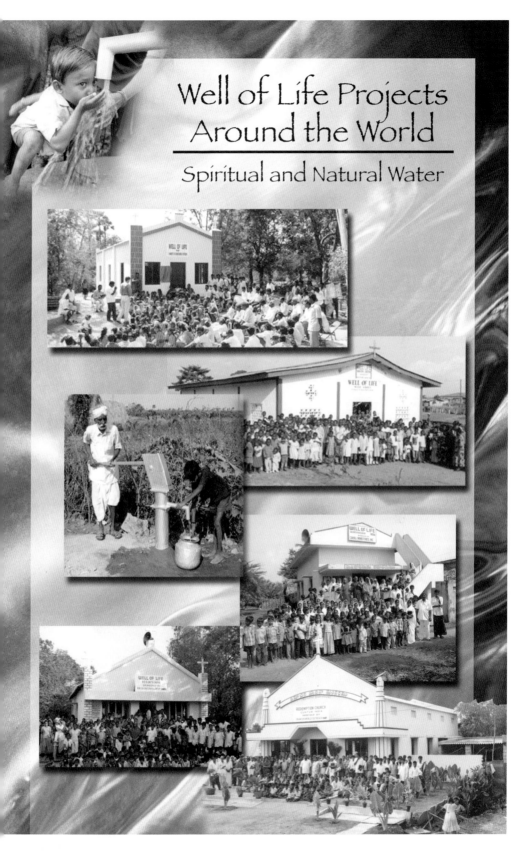

Well of Life Projects Around the World

Spiritual and Natural Water

Mobile Evangelism Unit

Empowering ministers to reach the remote villages of their Nation.

"So far because of the vehicle you donated to us in 1996 we have by God's grace planted 31 churches in Tanzania, 2 churches in the neighboring country of Rwanda, and 1 church in Uganda."

Pastor Eugene Marisa of Tanzania

M.E.U. ~ Costa Rica

M.E.U.s ~ Philippines

M.E.U.s ~ Tanzania

An "M.E.U." consists of a vehicle, P.A. system, and a film projector.

Mobile Evangelism Unit

To date 82 M.E.U.s, plus 100s of motorcycles and bicycles have been given.

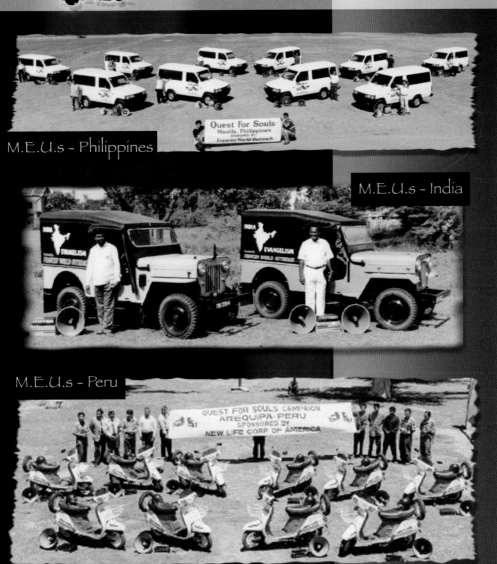

M.E.U.s ~ Philippines

Quest For Souls
Manila, Philippines
SPONSORED BY
Frances World Outreach

M.E.U.s ~ India

M.E.U.s ~ Peru

QUEST FOR SOULS CAMPAIGN
AREQUIPA, PERU
SPONSORED BY
NEW LIFE CORP OF AMERICA

Taking the message of Jesus Christ into the villages and towns where most would not venture.

Mobile Evangelism Unit

Our goal is to provide 100 mobile evangelism units to 100 different nations.

M.E.U.s - Liberia

M.E.U.s - India

QUEST FOR SOULS CAMPAIGN
INDIA

M.E.U. - Uganda

It is one of the most highly effective tools used by native ministers.

In John 9:7, Jesus told a blind man, "Go, wash in the pool of Siloam." *Doing* what he was told to do, the man was healed. He came back seeing. He moved his stone.

In Matthew 8:13, Jesus told a Roman centurion who asked healing for his servant, "Go your way...." As he went, "...his servant was healed that same hour." He moved his stone.

Again, in Matthew 17:27, Jesus told Peter how to answer their need for money to pay their taxes:

> ...go to the sea, cast in a hook, and take the fish that comes up first. And when you have opened its mouth, you will find a piece of money; take that and give it to them for Me and you.

Peter acted on the words of Jesus. He went fishing and used the proceeds to meet his tax obligation. He moved his stone!

Your miracle is in the cave behind the stone. The miracles for your ministry are in the cave behind the stone. To cause the release of the miracles in your life and ministry, you must move the stone. You move the stone by *doing* the Word of God.

The Bible says:

> Therefore, since we are *receiving a kingdom which cannot be shaken*, let us have grace, by which we may serve God....

> Hebrews 12:28

The King we serve cannot be shaken. His kingdom cannot be shaken. His royal decree, His Holy Word, cannot be shaken.

Faith is "birthed in the heart of the believer as he or she reads and meditates on the living Word of God. Faith is demonstrated as the believer acts on that Word."

It is faith that moves the hand of God. God will honor His Word. Will you?

If I pray for 100 sick people and they all die, what will I do? Tomorrow, I will go find another 100 to pray for. *Do* what God has told you to do, and let God do what He told you He would do.

GOD NEVER CONSULTS YOUR PAST

God never consults your past to determine your future.

Lot, the nephew of Abraham, left for Sodom and Gomorrah with his wife and two daughters. In defiance of God's command, his wife looked back and turned into a pillar of salt.

Lot's two daughters took him into a cave and had sex with their own father. As a result of this encounter, they bore children, one of which was named Moab (cursed). Jeremiah chapter 48 states that *everything* in Moab is cursed, and that Moab would wallow in its own vomit; there would be no dancing or rejoicing in Moab.

A Jewish farmer took his wife, Naomi, and their two sons to Moab because of the famine in Bethlehem. Their sons married Moabite girls. One of Naomi's daughters-in-law, Ruth, later married Boaz. Ruth and Boaz were the parents of Obed, the father of Jesse. Jesse brought forth David the king. David ushered in Jesus, the Son of the living God.

Ruth was a Moabite girl raised in the vomit of heathenism. Who was Boaz? He came through the loins of a temple prostitute by the name of Rahab. God brought Ruth and Boaz together. *God never consults your past to determine your future!*

God took a fearful, cowering, doubting, denying group of disciples and transformed them into powerful, faith filled, fearless men and women who evangelized the entire known world in just 200 years. *God never consults your past to determine your future.*

Act like you know God!

We *must* go to the nations with the miracle power of God. The disciples evangelized *their* world. They did not do it through silver-tongued oratory, human strategies, or cleverly designed church programs. They went beyond merely preaching and teaching in the pulpit.

The believers in the Early Church went forth into their communities in a demonstration of the miracle power of God.

We must do the same. *A miracle settles the issue.* Just do it and let God honor both your wisdom and your mistakes. Act like a man. Act like you know God!

CHAPTER FIFTEEN

A PERSUADING FORCE

The stage was set. This would be the first crusade of this kind in the history of the city. Anticipation and apprehension walk hand in hand during the days and weeks prior to the crusade. Anticipation because the populous of the city has been exposed to our crusades via television and videos. Apprehension because such an event has never happened here before. "Will the same things happen in this place?" is the thought that plagues the minds of those involved.

The city we will focus on here is Arequipa, Peru. For centuries this place had been steeped in religion. Tradition passed down for generations had ruled the ways of Peru's second largest city. Our citywide miracle crusade would be the very first of this kind ever conducted in Arequipa. Catholicism claimed a staggering 95% of the population; the hand full of churches could boast a Christian population of only 1,500 in this city of over 400,000 people.

The Melgar stadium was chosen as the venue for the "Cruzada de Milagros." This landmark was well known for the popular soccer matches, but this place had never endured the battle that would transpire this week. This would be a battle for eternity's sake.

People are creatures of habit. Centuries of religious tradition is not easily forsaken to embrace—something radically new. Yet we were on a quest for precious souls. I knew that this city had the right to see and experience God in all His fullness, but would they come and embrace the Truth we presented. Like the Apostle Paul in I Corinthians we did not come with "enticing words of man's wisdom, but in demonstration of the spirit."

Thousands of posters decorated the walls. Scores of handbills were distributed. Banners stretched across key locations of the town, and newspapers heralded the event. There would be a crusade, and a curious crowd of onlookers the first night.

I took a text from Acts 3:1–8 and proclaimed the miracle wrought in the name of Jesus. My message: The Truth Shall Set You Free! The results of the liberating Gospel message began to flood the stage to testify. Blind eyes were opened, deaf ears could hear, and tumors dissolved in a moment's time. Suddenly, an empty wheelchair was being passed over the heads of the people, as the cripple woman walked. A wave of faith and excitement swept across the sea of people. Doubt and unbelief gave way as Jesus confirmed His Word with great signs and wonders.

The Truth Shall Set You Free!

The next day the city was buzzing with excitement. More people came and the miracles continued. Skeptics could not disclaim that which was taking place in their city. One lady, Mrs. Santos, suffered with Parkinson's disease for fifteen years and she received an instant miracle. She shook uncontrollably for years, now in an instant she was free.

Catholic priests, and even a Catholic bishop, were interviewed by the press. They were asked their opinion of our Gospel crusade.

Their response was printed on the front page of the largest newspaper—"We cannot deny the miracles," was their recorded statement. The city of Arequipa could not deny the miracles, they could not deny the absolute Lordship of Jesus Christ. Religion slowly bowed its knee as signs and wonders proved a persuading force in Arequipa.

WE CANNOT DENY IT

Now as they spoke to the people, the priests, the captain of the temple, and the Sadducees came upon them, being greatly disturbed that they taught the people and preached in Jesus the resurrection from the dead. And they laid hands on them, and put [them] in custody until the next day, for it was already evening. However, many of those who heard the word believed; and the number of the men came to be about five thousand.

And it came to pass, on the next day, that their rulers, elders, and scribes, as well as Annas the high priest, Caiaphas, John, and Alexander, and as many as were of the family of the high priest, were gathered together at Jerusalem. And when they had set them in the midst, they asked, "By what power or by what name have you done this?" Then Peter, filled with the Holy Spirit, said to them, "Rulers of the people and elders of Israel: If we this day are judged for a good deed [done] to a helpless man, by what means he has been made well, let it be known to you all, and to all the people of Israel, that by the name of Jesus Christ of Nazareth, whom you crucified, whom God raised from the dead, by Him this man stands here before you whole. This is the stone which was rejected by you builders, which has become the chief cornerstone. Nor is there salvation in any other, for there is no other name under heaven given among men by which we must be saved!" Now when they saw the boldness of Peter and John, and perceived that they were uneducated and untrained men, they marveled. And they realized that they had been with Jesus. And seeing the man who had been healed standing with them, they could say nothing against it.

But when they had commanded them to go aside out of the council, they conferred among themselves, saying, "What shall we do to these men? For, indeed, that a notable miracle has been done through them [is] evident to all who dwell in Jerusalem, and WE CANNOT DENY IT. But so that it spreads no further among the people, let us severely threaten them, that from now on they speak to no man in this name!" And they called them and commanded them not to speak at all nor teach in the name of Jesus. But Peter and John answered and said to them, "Whether it is right in the sight of God to listen to yon more than to God, you judge. For we cannot but speak the things which we have seen and heard!" So when they had further threatened them, they let them go, finding no way of punishing them, because of the people, since they all glorified God for what had been done. For the man was over forty years old on whom this miracle of healing had been performed.

Acts 4:1-22

Mere words can be disputed, divers doctrines can be argued, but a miracle cannot be denied. The undeniable miracle on this man who was over forty years of age gave credence to the message Peter proclaimed. Many did not want to hear. The religious figures devised ways to rid their city of the disciples presence. Yet many believed on Jesus because of the miracle. Even the most reveled religious pontificates had to confess—"We cannot deny it."

And this gospel of the kingdom shall be preached in all the world for a witness unto all nations; and then shall the end come.

Matthew 24:14

The words "for a witness" mean "with evidence"—miraculous or supernatural evidence. This is God's indispensable method of evangelizing the world and of turning the heathen to Christ.

And they went out and preached everywhere, the Lord working with [them] and confirming the word through the accompanying signs. Amen.

Mark 16:20

As Jesus proclaimed the kingdom of God, His words were confirmed by miracles. Throughout the book of Acts the disciples delivered the Gospel message, miracles confirmed that heaven backed their witness. To enter the arena of world evangelism without the demonstration and power of God confirming the preaching, is equivalent to entering into a mighty war void of weapons. Futility and meager results will be the vague impression you leave. When the Gospel of Jesus Christ is confirmed with signs and wonders the city will proclaim: Surely God is here and Jesus is His Son—WE CANNOT DENY IT!

GOOD NEWS

> The Spirit of the Lord is upon Me, because He has anointed Me to preach the GOSPEL to the poor; He has sent me TO HEAL the brokenhearted, to PROCLAIM LIBERTY to the captives and recovery of SIGHT TO THE BLIND, to SET AT LIBERTY those who are oppressed; to PROCLAIM the acceptable year of the Lord.
>
> Luke 4:18-19

God's anointing is upon GOOD NEWS. He never said He would anoint bad news. Bad news is to tell a sinner he is going to hell. That is not the Gospel. A sinner is well aware of that fact. The Good News is that Christ has made provision for them to have eternal life, hell can be avoided and their life one that is filled with God's goodness and abundance.

The world is cluttered with prophets of doom. The heralders of religion, tradition, and condemnation lie in wait, ready to spew their venom. With gritted teeth and a clenched fist they think they offer eternal hope. There is no anointing on bad news. The Spirit of the Lord has anointed me to preach the GOSPEL—GOOD NEWS. It is the goodness of God that leads to repentance. (Rom. 2:4)

What caused the paralyzed man to tear the roof off a house in order to get to Jesus? Good News. What caused the woman with an issue of blood to seek out Jesus, and press through the crowd? Good News. What drew the two blind men out of their homes in order to fumble their way to the Master's presence? Good News. What delivered the man's son who was often times cast into the fire by demon spirits? Good News.

People today are not interested in a doctoral dissertation. They will not sit and listen to a theological debate. The world will not be won by our suave demeanor as we enlighten the hearers with the "deeper truths" of God's Word. The world hungers for GOOD NEWS.

> **Then Philip went down to the city of Samaria and preached Christ (Good News) unto them... And there was great joy in that city.**
>
> ACTS 8:5-8

People today strive to make that which is simple, complicated and the pure, muddied. The Gospel message is a liberating one, but it is rendered powerless if delivered in a manner that it was never intended to be. Pure and simple. Good News. The Gospel.

I fear, lest somehow, as the serpent deceived Eve by his craftiness, so your minds may be corrupted for the SIMPLICITY THAT IS IN CHRIST.

2 Corinthians 11:3

Presented in simplicity the Gospel is powerful. The anointing is wrapped up in the Gospel. "His is such a simple word," they say, "He did not expound on any new revelations of the Word at all." No Greek, no Hebrew.

It doesn't take an hour of Greek word studies to present powerful Gospel truth. I suppose the message that Jesus brought on the cross to the thief hanging along side Him was a short one, but it was Good News. "Today you will be with me in paradise." That was Good News.

"Take up thy bed and walk" was Good News. "Receive thy sight," was Good News. "Be thou made whole"—Good News. "Come," is Good News. "Roll away the stone"—Good News. "Talithacumi," was Good News. "Silver and gold have I none, but that which I have give I thee. In the name of Jesus Christ of Nazareth rise up and walk," is Good News. Nothing deep. Nothing profound. Just Good News.

CHAPTER SIXTEEN

SEEDED FOR SOULS

The faces of people, their images, have been etched upon my heart and mind. For twenty-five years, in over ninety countries of the world, I have had the mounted honor of ministering to millions of people face to face in huge open-air campaigns.

I have often sat in airports, walked in the forgotten villages, and traveled the so-called roads of the nations of this world, when a certain individual will grasp the focus of my attention. Suddenly my thoughts will enter their world, and I find myself contemplating their eternal fate.

Some of those faces have never left me. I can close my eyes and see them just as plain as if they were standing right in front of me. Time and time again I ask myself—"Who will reach them if not me?" Dear friend of Christ, most of the world knows nothing of the redemptive plan of Christ. "WHO WILL REACH THEM IF NOT YOU?"

THE EARTH IS THE LORD'S

The earth is the Lord's and all its fullness, the world and those who dwell therein.

Psalm 24:1

In one of my international adventures, I had the rare opportunity to attend, and document on film, a modem day voodoo service. Here these devotees to demon spirits sacrificed animals, mutilated their bodies, and embraced evil spirits.

I have witnessed the epitome of idol worship in the nation of India. In this complex country of nearly one billion people, the Hindus claim to have more than 300 million gods. Eighty seven percent of India's inhabitants are Hindu.

In China there are nearly one billion people who know only communism as god. And in the world today, three billion do not know Christ.

A valid question posed to God is this: "If all those who dwell on the earth are Yours, then why is there seemingly so much evidence to the contrary?"

God's response—"The earth is mine, in the same manner that Canaan belonged to Israel—it is rightfully owned, but un-possessed. The latter is your responsibility." Who will reach them?

LADIES & GENTLEMEN, PLEASE TAKE YOUR SEATS

You prepare a table for me in the presence of my enemies...

Psalms 23:5

Many today seek refuge inside the four walls of their church. Surrounded by saints singing praises to the Most High, they cling to another psalm which says, *"Do not gather my soul with sinners."*

(Ps. 26:9). How is it that so many seem oblivious to the world around them and the appointment of cause to their lives?

We do not partake of the world's ways, but we must NOT forsake those whose eternity is trapped but not yet solidified.

Sinners do not go to church. Thus, Christ commands us to "Go into the highways and byways and compel them to come in." We revel in the comfort of friendly sanctified faces. Yet His marching orders send us into their world.

Face the fear of the personal witness. Share your faith. Some must accept the challenge and dare to tread upon enemy territory.

> *Apparent disaster is the doorway to opportunity.*

No fear. Apparent disaster is the doorway to opportunity. There, God is preparing a table for you in the presence of your enemies. Exploiting crisis situations He will turn criticism and adversity into food for us to feast upon.

God will celebrate you in the presence of your enemies. Who will reach them if not you? Possibly no one.

THE CALL, VISION, AND CHALLENGE

Behold I say to you, lift up your eyes and look at the fields, for they are already white for harvest!

John 4:35

I am astounded at the vast number of Bible school graduates each year who walk away with a diploma in their hand, nonsense in their head, and nothing in their hearts.

These students invest years of their lives and upon completion of the required courses they ask themselves—WHAT NOW? Months, years, and for some a lifetime is far spent "waiting on God." Wondering what their call is and what they are to do, they do nothing of consequence.

To those struggling with direction for your life, take a close look at John 4:35. Encapsulated in this verse is a call, vision, and challenge with enough passion to propel you into fruitful ministry.

> **Behold I say to you, (The Call) lift up your eyes and look at the fields, (TheVision) for they are already white for harvest. (The Challenge)**
>
> John 4:35

In Matthew 13:38 Jesus said, *"The field is the world."* There is your call, vision, challenge, and direction. Who will reach them if not you? Maybe no one.

THE VALLEY OF DECISION

> **Put in the sickle, for the harvest is ripe...Multitudes, multitudes in the valley of decision...**
>
> Joel 3:13-14

In countries such as the United States, it is quite easy for the body of Christ to become lulled into a sense of accomplishment for a job well done. Airwaves are filled with the Gospel message, and pastors and evangelists almost trip over one another vying for pulpit opportunities.

It's a different story in the West African nation of Sierra Leone. Ancestor worship and pagan rituals have these unknowing people talking to the dead and conducting the bloody act of female circumcision. Witch doctors are sought out by many for answers to the questions of life. The sadistic ceremonies have the demon possessed adherents driving spears through their flesh. Another will cut off his tongue, throw it on the ground, then reattach the severed appendage.

Muslim neighbors to the north have their sights set on winning these people to their cause. They are in the valley of decision. They will respond to the Gospel message, but how will they hear without a preacher? Who will reach them if not you? Maybe no one.

ASK AND IT SHALL BE GIVEN YOU

Ask, and it will be given to you; seek, and you will find; knock, and it will be opened to you.

Matthew 7:7

As a child of God we have been given a precious covenant with the Father. It is our birthright, as a child of God, to receive the benefits of our salvation. Miracle healing and health is ours. Abundant provision and protection is the divine order for our lives.

Jesus spoke very plainly and told us to "ASK." And with this particular promise we are very quick to comply. We storm heaven and bombard the throne with our requests. "Lord bless me, heal my body, let thy favor envelope my life. Father you know my financial situation and how I desperately need your intervention," we pray.

Fine. After all, Jesus told us to ask. The heart of God relishes our dependence upon Him. BUT HAVE YOU EVER ASKED GOD FOR A PASSION FOR SOULS?

> **Ask of Me, and I will give you the heathen for your inheritance. The ends of the earth for your possession.**
>
> **Psalm 2:8**

Ask God for a passion for souls. Who will reach them if not you? Perhaps no one will.

EVERYONE IS LOOKING FOR YOU

> **Then He healed many who were sick with various diseases, and cast out many demons... Now in the morning... He prayed. And Simon and those who were with Him searched for Him. When they found Him, they said to Him, *"Everyone is looking for You."* but He said to them, *"Let us go into the next towns, that I may preach there also, because for this purpose I have come forth."***
>
> **Mark 1:34-38**

To hear the words, "Everyone is looking for you" is near utopia for ministers today. To mount the platform in a place where you are celebrated and loved, by those who have filled the place to overflowing, is paradise for the man of God.

Here Jesus was, in the midst of revival. Miracles were happening, and the multitudes responded to his love. In the midst of this outpouring Jesus said, "There are others that must hear."

I have made it my aim to preach the Gospel, not where Christ was named...

Romans 15:20

We are to be fishers of men, not keepers of the aquarium. Who will reach them if not you? No one.

TOMORROW

Now is the accepted time, today is the day of salvation.

2 Corinthians 6:2

IN THE MIDST OF A MIRACLE

...the keeper of the prison... drew his sword and was about to kill himself. But Paul called with a loud voice...and immediately he and all his family were baptized.

Acts 16:27-33

At midnight Paul and Silas were singing praises unto God while they were in prison. The doors flew open and God provided a miracle escape plan. The keeper of the prison was about to take his own life, fearing he had failed in his duties.

In the midst of their miracle Paul seized the opportunity to bring salvation to the jail keeper. That one man's conversion caused an entire family to receive Jesus.

Rejoicing in our miracles we get caught up with a great joy of His presence in our lives.

How often have opportunities been lost to present the Gospel as we were too nearsighted to realize them. In the midst of your miracles, God has set a keeper of a prison before you. In the midst of financial miracles, you can touch eternity.

Your physical miracle will present a platform for you, not only to rejoice over God's touch, but to touch eternity of those who look on.

In the midst of a miracle there is a Philippian jailer. In the midst of an earthquake a family awaits. Clothed in many robes, disguised in many faces, people await the Gospel truth. Who will reach them if not you?

MILLIONS HELD HOSTAGE

The Lord is not slack concerning His promise, as some count slackness, but is longsuffering toward us, not willing that any should perish but that all should come to repentance.

2 Peter 3:9

I once heard Lester Sumrall make two very powerful statements. He said, *"The devil wants you to do good, because doing good will keep you from doing God's best. And God's best is souls."* And, *"If you keep souls as your number one priority you will never be out of the will of God."*

The great missionary statesman Oswald J. Smith once said, *"No one should hear the Gospel twice, before everyone has had the chance to hear it once."*

Soul conscious. A heart for the lost. A passion for souls. These attitudes are the ones that had forged the lives of the heroes of the faith.

Today a jumbo jet can be hijacked with 80 people on board. An event such as this would grab headlines the world over.

The fact that millions are held hostage by eternal darkness, with hell being their plight, is barely mentioned by the body of Christ today.

Jesus gave His life a "ransom for many." God had one Son, and He made Him a missionary.

What attitude governs your thoughts? What passion directs your finances? What heart portrays your ambition in life?

Who will reach them if not you? Perhaps no one will.

THE MIRACLE OF THE MOMENT

He (Jesus) left Judea and departed again to Galilee.

John 4:3

Too often we fumble through existence, missing out on life. Those in the body of Christ today are almost completely "event" oriented. They rush from project to project, function to function, and service to service.

Many today await the opening day of the next camp meeting. They endure the days until the next scheduled church gathering.

With great anticipation and enduring agony, they survive another mundane day.

Rushing to the next event many miss the MIRACLE OF THE MOMENT. We miss out on life waiting for the next event.

In John 4:3 Jesus was on a mission. The Spirit was sending Him to Galilee. But in John 4:4 the Bible says, *"BUT HE HAD TO GO THROUGH SAMARIA!"*

What happened in Samaria, on the way to Galilee? He met the woman at the well, **and many Samaritans from that city believed in Him. (vs. 39)**

What is the miracle of the moment? It is Christ in YOU, the hope of glory. Jesus wants you to give your life to Him 365 days a year—plus leap year.

On the way to your next event, or service, you must pass through your Samaria. Do not miss the miracle of the moment. Christ in you is the hope of glory.

REGIONS BEYOND

To preach the gospel in the regions beyond you...

2 Corinthians 10:16

Today there are at least 3.8 billion people alive on planet earth who are on their way to hell. If you allow one foot per person in a single file line, and compress the line so tight that not even a piece of paper could fit between the individuals, that line would reach around the world TWENTY FIVE TIMES.

Think of it. A line of precious people, that reaches twenty five times around the world, marching into eternal darkness.

Oswald J. Smith said, *"Our duty is not done when we minister only to those who come into our churches. If they do not come, we have no choice but to go to them."*

In the light of the enormous task of reaching the world, our lives become much bigger and more significant than car payments and petty doctrinal differences.

Pastor Larry Stockstill writes, *"Most churches and individuals are so embroiled in debt and activities that the mammoth project of reaching the world becomes the task of a small committee rather than the very life-flow and thrill of the local church."*

The Apostle Paul made it his mission and passion to preach in "regions beyond." We must go outside the church, out where the sinners are.

HIDING PLACE OF HIS POWER

And His brightness was as the light; He had rays coming out of His hand; and there was the hiding place of His power.

Habakkuk 3:4

During World War II, a bombing raid pelted a small village in France. As a tribute to their faith in God, a large stone statue of Jesus stood in the center of the village. The exploding artillery left the beautiful statue of Jesus in many pieces.

The towns people were brokenhearted when they gathered the next morning and saw the sculpture in ruins. With great determination they meticulously began to put the broken pieces of Jesus back together. It was like working a puzzle as they fit each piece into its proper place.

As they neared the completion of the project every piece was found and properly reattached, but the hands of Jesus were no where to be found. The beautiful statue of Christ once again stood in the village square, but there were no hands on the arms that were stretched out wide.

Someone had an idea, and he had a bronze plaque attached to the statue, engraved with these words: I HAVE NO HANDS BUT YOUR HANDS!

God has no hands but yours...

God has no hands, but yours. YOU are God's hands extended. His voice on this earth. His compassion revealed. His power is hidden in YOU. The cause of Christ is ours to fulfill.

CHAPTER SEVENTEEN

A PASSION FOR SOULS

I have made more than twenty-six trips to the great nation of India, but I do not think it is possible to become accustomed to the sights one beholds. The consequences of sin are blatantly obvious, and the hopelessness of "religion" is personified throughout.

This country boasts an enormous population of nearly one billion people, yet only one percent are Christians.

The Gospel has already taken me to over ninety countries of the world. Few of those countries fare any better than this land of India in their stand for Christ. In the midst of this realization, I have to continually ask myself, "Where is your heart?" To the Body of Christ, of which you are a part, God would also ask, "Where is your heart?"

The fact that there are nearly three billion people in the world who have not heard the Gospel of Jesus Christ is *an indictment against the Church*. The fact that Christians made up a little less than thirty percent of the world's population in 1868, and one hundred years later a little less than thirty-two percent is *an indictment against the Church*.

The painful realization that only one percent of the monies that come into U.S. churches ever go to world missions *is an indictment against the Church*.

The amazing information that has come to light that tells us that Islam is the second-largest religion in the world, the fastest-growing religion worldwide, and the fastest-growing religion in the United States at this moment is an indictment against the Church.

Staggering statistics of a world that is racing toward a Christ-less eternity with seemingly little intervention from the Body of Christ has mounted up as evidence against us.

The charge, the one task—yea, the command—that Christ left the Church as The Great Commission has been ignored.

The verdict, if it were handed down today, would have to read guilty, because of the irrefutable evidence against her. The sentence has already been prescribed in Ezekiel 3:18–19 (New King James Version):

> When I say to the wicked, "You shall surely die," and you give him no warning, nor speak to warn the wicked from his wicked way, to save his life, that same wicked man shall die in his iniquity; but his blood I will require at your hand.
>
> Yet, if you warn the wicked, and he does not turn from his wickedness, nor from his wicked way, he shall die in his iniquity; but you have delivered your soul.

The penalty is that the blood of lost humanity will be on our hands. Some will cry, "Foul, foul! That is the Old Testament, formed under the law, and we are not under the law."

Yet to that one who cries, "Innocent," I would direct your attention to the Apostle Paul in the New Testament, who carried the weight of Ezekiel 3 right into New Testament times, as we see in this passage from Acts.

When Silas and Timothy had come from Macedonia,
Paul was constrained by the Spirit, and testified to
the Jews that Jesus is the Christ.

But when they opposed him, and blasphemed, he
shook his garments and said to them, "Your blood be
upon your own hands; I am clean. From now on I
will go to the Gentiles."

Acts 18:5-6

God is demanding that the Church stop being busy and start
being effective. A mandate from the Almighty has been ordered:

> *God is demanding that the Church stop being busy and start being effective.*

Lost humanity must be presented
with the light of the Gospel! Souls
by the millions now sit in darkness, at the door of death.

Today, many have Ph.D.
degrees and doctorates of divinity,
but they have no heart. Every time
the pendulum of your clock
swings, someone who is ignorant
of Christ's salvation gasps in hopeless despair—their plight, a Christless eternity!

About one million people in
the world die each week without Christ. Does this mean nothing
to you? Have we a pain in our hearts for perishing men and
women? Are you haunted day and night with the thought that millions are perishing on every side, that multitudes are going down
to the regions of despair, without one ray of hope?

When a man has been endued with power from on high, he will have a burden for souls. Boast no more of your anointing if you do not love souls.

The burden for souls—how it has characterized God's anointed ones throughout the centuries! We must be persuaded that apart from the salvation of souls, the Church has no grounds for her existence.

Where is your heart, man or woman of God? Preachers who should be fishing for men are too often fishing for compliments from men. Where is your heart?

According to Christ, we have only one mission: to save souls. Yet they perish. Think of them—hundreds of millions, one thousand million eternal souls that need Christ!

Linking passion to evangelism, Leighton Ford, in his book, *The Christian Persuader,* writes:

"Before evangelism is a program, it is a passion—a passion of the heart which issues in saving action. Evangelism is the passion of Moses, 'Oh, this people have sinned...yet now, if thou wilt forgive their sin—if not, blot me, I pray thee, out of the book which thou hast written.'"

It is the passion of Paul, *"Woe is me if I preach not the Gospel."* It is the anguished cry of Jesus as he weeps over a doomed city, *"O Jerusalem, how oft would I have gathered thee."*

Evangelism is the cry of Knox, *"Give me Scotland or I die,"* and of Wesley, *"The world is my parish."* Evangelism is Henry Martyn landing on the shores of India and crying, *"Here let me burn out for God!"* It is David Brainerd coughing up blood from his tubercular lungs as he prays in the snow for the Indians. It is George

Whitefield crossing the Atlantic thirteen times in a small boat to preach in the American Colonies.

Is there a passion for souls that grips your heart? Does this heart for the lost dictate your thoughts, actions, and pursuits? Can anything but a genuine passion and quest for souls merit the focus of our attention and intentions?

Our goal is nothing less than the penetration of the whole world with the Gospel message.

When we get humble enough, low enough, desperate enough, hungry enough, concerned enough, passionate enough, broken enough, clean enough, and prayerful enough, God will send us a revival that equals and surpasses any awakening the Church has ever known.

Preachers young and old, the rookies and the veterans in the faith, laymen and Sunday school workers alike, perpetually bombard the gates of heaven, ever asking, pleading, and begging, "Lord, let me do your will."

God's will is summed up in one powerful scripture: *"The Lord is... not willing that any should perish..."* (2 Peter 3:9).

We can surmise that God's will is that all people should come to how His saving grace, for 2 Peter 3:9 tells us that God is not willing that any should perish.

Lester Sumrall once said, *"If you put souls as your number one priority, you will never be out of the will of God."*

The devil loves for us to do good things, because doing good things is what keeps us from doing God's best: reaching souls.

Our passion for souls, and the urgency to the mission is that of the Christian ambassador who is under strict orders from his sovereign King.

A VOICE FOR SOULS

Peter and John are with Christ at the Transfiguration, when Peter says, "Master, this is wonderful! I have never had such a grand experience in all my life. I want to stay here forever. Let's build three tabernacles so we can stay and dwell here. I want to enjoy this great experience all my life."

But suddenly the light fades, and Moses and Elijah disappear. As the disciples look up, they see no man, except Jesus.

Jesus says, "Let's go. This was good for the moment, but this is not what we are here for. There is much work to do. I have other sheep. The multitudes that are perishing must be reached. My message is for the whole world. We must work the works of God while it is still day, for the night is coming when no man can work."

The life of Christ exemplifies a voice for souls. Jesus was never content abiding only among those who had already believed His words. He was on a constant quest for souls, a quest to reach out to those who had not yet heard; to those who would face eternal damnation without the Savior.

The life of Christ exemplifies a voice for souls.

In Genesis 18, Abraham was a voice for souls to his generation. He pleaded with God to spare a people. The apostle Paul was a voice for souls in his generation. He was not content to only "build up the saints" in places where his labor had already bore great fruit, but said, *"I have made it my aim to preach the Gospel, not where Christ was named..."* (Romans 15:20).

That is frontier evangelism at the heart—pioneers of the cross on a quest for souls.

What value do we place on a soul? We continually rejoice and give thanks because of our own salvation. We are grateful to God for the person or persons who brought the Gospel to us. *But what about those around us who are not saved?* What is the value of a soul to you?

God places supreme worth on every human soul.

> **For a soul is far too precious to be ransomed by mere earthly wealth.**
>
> **There is not enough of it in all the earth to buy eternal life for just one soul, to keep it out of hell.**
>
> Psalm 49:8-9 TLB

> **For what is a man profited, if he shall gain the whole world, and lose his own soul? Or what shall a man give in exchange for his soul?**
>
> Matthew 16:26

Jesus Christ is the urgency of evangelism. This fact was grippingly apparent in the life of Paul the apostle. He was a Christ-centered, Christ-mastered, Christ-intoxicated man who penned the missionary motivational writings in Second Corinthians 5:10–21.

In these verses, Paul indicates that the secret of his passion for souls lay in three realms. In each, Christ was supreme.

First, there is the realm of theology—the Christ-centered mind. These verses are packed with profound statements and phrases: "the judgment seat of Christ," "the terror of the Lord," "one died for all," "God was in Christ," "not imputing their trespasses," "the word of reconciliation," and "the righteousness of God."

Obviously, Paul's passion for souls was not merely an emotion: it was deeply thought out and contemplated.

HOW SHALL THEY GO, EXCEPT THEY BE SENT?

As building funds swell, missions' budgets continue to become more and more anemic. It is when missions are neglected that churches have to turn to glorified begging and garage sales.

Where is your heart? Many talk a good conscience—millions of dollars are spent each year talking about missions—yet the Spirit of God is calling us to action.

We have been bumping our heads on the tithe as the ceiling in Christian giving. We have made tithes the ceiling rather than the foundation for our giving.

If we tithed all our possessions in the light of the judgment seat; if we preached every sermon with one eye on damned humanity and the other on the judgment seat; if we gave beyond what is deemed as an obligation to give, we would have a Holy Spirit revival that would shake the earth and liberate millions of precious souls.

Nehemiah 8:10 reads, *"Go your way, eat the fat, and drink the sweet, and send portions unto them for whom nothing is prepared..."* Portions for those for whom nothing is prepared represents the un-evangelized world.

Called of God, have you ever set aside from your abundance a portion to reach the un-reached of your generation? A careful look at Nehemiah 10:32–39 will unveil the concept of a faith promise offering.

Have you ever considered giving such an offering, where you make a promise that is just between you and God, and believe Him to bring that desired amount to you so souls may be won?

The Gospel is free, but the pipeline to get the Gospel to those who have not yet heard costs money *"How shall they preach, except they be sent?"* (Romans 10:15). They cannot.

In the Body of Christ, though many boast of great faith, most are so busy studying what they do not have that they do not see what they do *have*.

In the hands of Jesus, a lunch of two fish and five loaves fed five thousand. Two cakes produced many meals, and a few stones in the hands of a believer slew a giant. See what you have. Look at the possibilities. A world can be won!

SEVEN REASONS FOR MISSIONS

Reason 1. The Bible commands it. *"And He said to them, 'Go into all the world and preach the Gospel to every creature.'"* (Mark 16:15).

Reason 2. Love compels it. *"For God so loved the world that He gave His only begotten Son, that whoever believes in Him should not perish but have everlasting life"* (John 3:16).

Reason 3. Fairness requires it. Oswald J. Smith said, *"Why should anyone hear the Gospel twice, before everyone has had the chance to hear it once?"*

Reason 4. Hope demands it. *"It was through what his Son did that God cleared a path for everything to come to him—all things in heaven and on earth—for Christ's death on the cross has made peace with God for all by his blood"* (Colossians 1:20 TLB). *"...Christ in you, the hope of glory"* (Colossians 1:27). It is Christ in you the hope of someone else getting into glory.

Reason 5. Believers owe it. Paul wrote, *"I am a debtor both to Greeks and to barbarians, both to wise and to unwise. So, as much as is in me, I am ready to preach the Gospel to you..."* (Romans 1:14–15).

Reason 6. Jesus awaits it. *"And this Gospel of the kingdom will be preached in all the world as a witness to all the nations, and then the end will come"* (Matthew 24:14).

Reason 7. Souls are worth it. *"What profit is there if you gain the whole world—and lose eternal life? What can be compared with the value of eternal life?"* (Matthew 16:26 TLB).

The command to go into all the world was not just directed to a small band of believers 2,000 years ago. It is a command that has resounded throughout the history of the Church. This challenge has echoed throughout the hearts of God's servants for centuries and will continue to be declared until God's final trumpet blast.

Does it make sense? Is it cost-effective and wise to send missionaries? Could the money be better spent on supporting only nationals, or in other ways?

Questions like these come dangerously close to the question asked by Judas as the precious ointment was poured upon Jesus' feet. God is a God of great abundance. No limiting force has capped His resources. It is much better to simply obey than to try to rationalize the logic of His instructions.

God-fashioned, God-filled, and God-fired. The two prerequisites for successful Christian living are vision and passion. Where there is no vision, the people perish. Where there is no passion, the Church perishes.

Alexander Duff, the veteran missionary to India, returned home to Scotland after many years' service, to die. In great feebleness he stood before the Presbyterian assembly and pleaded for missionaries for India.

In the midst of his appeal, he fainted and was taken into another room. After a doctor had worked on him for a long time, he finally regained consciousness. When he realized where he was, he said, "I didn't finish my appeal; take me back and let me fish it!" The doctor told him it would be a great risk to his life to try to go back now, but he replied, "I'll do it if I die."

So they helped the old, white-haired missionary into the assembly hall, and as he appeared at the door, they all sprang to their feet as one man to greet him, and then sat down and listened in tearful and breathless silence to that grand old hero of the cross.

With a trembling voice he said, "Fathers and mothers of Scotland, is it true that you have no more sons to send to India? There is money in the bank to send them, but where are the laborers who will go into the field? When Queen Victoria calls for volunteers for her army in India, you freely give your sons and say nothing about the trying climate of the land. But when the Lord Jesus calls for volunteers, you say, 'We have no more sons to give.'"

Then, turning to the moderator of the assembly, he said, "Mr. Moderator, if it is true that Scotland has no more sons to give Christ for India, then, although I lost my health in that land and have come home to die, I will be off tomorrow and go back to the shores of the Ganges and lay my life down as a Scotsman who is ready to die for them."

That, dear friends, is a passion for souls! The seed is the Word, and the field is the world. We cannot make the seed grow, but we are called, each and every one, to see that the seed is scattered over the whole field. The goal is penetration. Evangelism is not a sporadic mishap, but a continuous engagement with the world at every level of society.

Every son and daughter of the king has received a decree to bring His voice to where it is yet to be heard: His light to where it shines dimly.

Do not put a question mark where God has put a period. Break away from the "norm." Many claim to be sound in their doctrine. They are sound, but they are sound asleep! The early Church "moved." In moving, something or someone must be left behind.

It does not take an entire denomination to impact a nation. God has always furthered His cause with the overwhelming minority. He has used small, passion-filled groups like Gideon's band of servants and the twelve disciples. He has used individuals like John G. Lake and T.L. Osborn to shape their generation worldwide.

God is too big for anyone to have a copyright on any project. Do what others have done that has worked, but be yourself. Elijah did not get a wig to be like Samson. Nor did he wait outside to see a burning bush.

Let a passion for souls dictate your pursuit to reach them. Jesus did not get excited about the multitude, nor discouraged with the one at the well. A quest for souls will bring you before the masses as well as before the one Ethiopian eunuch.

Be a voice for souls. John the Baptist raised a dead nation. He was a "voice." Most today are only echoes. If you listen closely, you will be able to tell what latest book they have read.

> *John the Baptist raised a dead nation. He was a "voice." Most today are only echoes.*

The great revivalist Leonard Ravenhill writes, *"It takes broken men to break men. We have equipment, but not enduement; commotion but not creation; action but not unction; rattle but not revival. We are dogmatic but not dynamic."*

Nothing greater is needed in this hour than a God-ordained, God-inspired, God-breathed passion for souls upon the body of Christ.

Worldwide exploration into un-chartered territories with the Word of God is the supreme need of the day.

I am on a quest for souls. Pushing staff and resources to the limits, my pursuit is global evangelism of the three billion people who have yet to hear the Gospel.

I do not want to flow in modern-day marketing strategies; I want to walk in the anointing. Where is your heart?

The whole earth shall see it and return to the Lord;
the people of every nation shall worship Him.

Psalm 22:27 TLB

Keep close to God. Keep close to people. Bring God and people together.

This is not a chapter of condemnation, but of hope, for God would never require such a task of us without the potential of our being able to fulfill it.

CHAPTER EIGHTEEN

THE PULPIT FAILS TO GRIP

Churchgoers, sermon-sick and teaching-tired, leave the meeting as they entered—visionless and passionless!

God is able to do exceedingly, abundantly above all that we ask or think, according to the power that works in us. God's problem today is not communism or liberalism; God's problem today is dead fundamentalism!

> *God's problem today is not communism or liberalism; God's problem today is dead fundamentalism!*

In stark contrast to today, our forefathers in the faith—the men and women God has instructed us to imitate—had a profound effect when they stood in their pulpits. Reading about them, you begin to sense a markedly different realm of ministry.

When Jonathan Edwards preached his memorable sermon, "Sinners in the Hands of an Angry God," God's power was so mightily poured out and His holiness so manifested that the elders threw their arms around the pillars of the church and cried, "Lord, save us; we are slipping down to hell!"

William Carey's 1792 sermon in Nottingham, England, when he preached, "Expect great things from God. Attempt great things for God," shook an entire Baptist denomination and birthed its missions program, which has continued to the present day. *One sermon!*

While in South Africa, Andrew Murray received an invitation to speak at a large convention in the United States. Rather than hurrying to purchase a ticket for the journey, he challenged himself: "Do I have a message for that meeting? Would I be able to deliver that message so clearly to make it worthwhile to go all that distance?"

Do ministers contemplate such things today, or do they jump at the slightest hint of interest shown in their ministry, knowing, having as their goal the offering they will receive?

What of the charge and statement of purpose John Wesley gave each Methodist minister when he told them they had *"nothing to do but save souls."* Could this have been the key to the momentous spread of the Gospel and the grip that Methodist ministers had on the world in the 1700s?

General William Booth, the founder of the Salvation Army, lived by this one set of principles: "Some men's passion is gold. Some men's passion is fame. *My passion is souls."* Is there any wonder why the Salvation Army has had such an influence?

Reading the memoirs of Rev. John Smith, you can easily sense the depth, purpose, and conviction which dictated his life's accomplishments. His attitude—"Give me souls, or else I die"—is what caused him to make a genuine impact on his world.

What about the life and ministry of Charles Finney? He reportedly brought more than 500,000 souls to Christ, and more than 85 percent of them remained in the faith until their death.

What passion so governed and directed his life that he was able to walk into a factory, unknown by anyone in that town, and every person in the factory fell to their knees and wept for mercy before God?

God's Word tells us to imitate fathers in the faith like them. From their pulpits, the Spirit of the Lord grabbed hold of people's hearts and drove them to their knees. An overwhelming passion for holiness, truth, and, ultimately, souls piloted their lives and ministries. That passion and hunger which governed their lives was prominent in their pulpits.

But, alas, today the pulpit fails to grip. Pastors and evangelists shrug off their responsibility and hurl accusations at the "cold, hard congregations" they address.

Who is to blame? Are we to attribute the lack of results in our ministries to the people's "hardness of heart"? Does the fault lie there? No, my fellow ministers and co-workers, the fault and blame must rest with us.

If we were what and where we should be, the signs and wonders would follow us, as they did our forefathers in the days of old.

I would suggest to you that every failure, every sermon that fails to grip and break the hearts of the people, every service where God's presence and miracles are not prevalent should drive us to our knees!

It should cause us, in all humility, to search our hearts. If our churches and meetings are cold and unresponsive, it is because we are cold. Like preacher, like people.

Does the minister grip, save, and convert by his message? I have begun to challenge my preaching. My preaching and prayer life had to be challenged by the outcome. Let each of

God's ministers challenge his own spirituality and ministry. What is the outcome? What are the results?

God emphatically states, "I have chosen you, and ordained you, that ye should go and bring forth fruit..." (John 15:16 KJV).

Study the Old Testament. Examine the four Gospels. Contemplate the lives of the members of the early church, as found in the Book of Acts. Meditate on the ministries of our forefathers in the faith.

Their lives were pure and holy. A zeal for God and a passion for souls permeated their beings. Miracles were in demonstration in their ministries.

Can we get the same results without following their example? If we can, then let us prove to the world that we have found a better way. But if not, then let us begin to follow those who through faith and patience have obtained the promises.

Before expecting God to move in our lives and grip the hearts of the hearers in our ministries, we will first have to deal with the question of sin. Unless our lives are right in the sight of God, we can pray from now until the Millennium, but revival will never come.

> **Your iniquities have separated between you and your God, and your sins have hid his face from you, that he will not hear.**
>
> Isaiah 59:2 KJV

> **If I regard iniquity in my heart, the Lord will not hear me.**
>
> Psalm 66:18 KJV

If my people, which are called by my name, shall humble themselves, and pray, and seek my face, and turn from their wicked ways; then will I hear from heaven....

2 Chronicles 7:14 KJV

Sin must be utterly forsaken. Mere remorse is not true, godly sorrow unto repentance. Judas, though filled with remorse, never repented. It is a broken and a contrite heart that must be presented before a holy God (Psalm 51:17).

Before this portion is dismissed with the attitude, "I'm right before God; I have not killed, committed adultery, taken the name of the Lord in vain, and I do not smoke or drink," let us look more closely into our hearts.

> *We look at the "big" sins, from which we practice complete abstinence, and forget the fact that in God's eyes, sin is sin, whether "big" or "small."*

We look at the "big" sins, from which we practice complete abstinence, and forget the fact that in God's eyes, sin is sin, whether "big" or "small."

We must challenge our lives and examine our hearts. Could it be that to neglect the Word of God is sin? Is the only time you open "the Book" to get a quick message for a meeting you are about to minister?

And what of prayerlessness, when we only go to God when finances reach a desperate state? Neglect of the many things we know we should or should not be doing could very well be the sin (obstacle) that is keeping us from being the man or woman God wishes to use and to promote His power.

We cannot pray, tithe, give, shout, or cry beyond our last act of disobedience. Sin must be dealt with and put away if we want to be God's channel of power.

What of the sin of *carelessness?* This generation of preachers is responsible for this generation of sinners! At the very doors of the churches are the masses—unwon because they are unreached. Unreached because they are unloved.

God says in His Word, *"When I say unto the wicked, Thou shalt surely die; and thou givest him not warning, nor speakest to warn the wicked from his wicked way, to save his life; the same wicked man shall die in his iniquity; but his blood will I require at thine hand"* (Ezekiel 3:18 KJV).

What are we *doing* to reach our community? What are we doing to reach the world and fulfill the Great Commission? If we do not consider world missions—if we do not pray, give, and go to nations abroad, we are telling nearly three billion people, "Die and go to hell, because I do not care."

We are telling the unreached people in Africa, "Die and go to hell, because I do not care." We are telling the unreached in South America and nearly 800 million unreached in India, "Die and go to hell, because *I do not care!"*

We cannot offer lip service with a resounding "I care." If you do not pray, give, and/or go, your actions and your life say that you do not care.

LOVE, AMERICAN STYLE

Only three-tenths of one percent of every dollar that comes into the church in America goes toward missionary evangelism. That does not impress me as fulfilling Jesus' priority for the Church.

In this modern era of technology, the American mindset is world evangelization via television. We must realize that in this thinking, we are seeing with a limited perspective, through American eyes.

In watching Christian television in the United States, one senses that the world is being won to Christ through their programming.

Access to these ministries in America is easy and abundant. Statistics show there is one television set for every 1.2 persons in the U.S., with Christian programming readily available 24 hours a day. Virtually every household within our borders has a television set. This is hardly the case in other countries.

In England, for example, there is one television set for every three persons. In Russia, the ratio is one television set for every 3.2 persons. In India, there is one television set for every 42 persons. (Only 1.6 percent of the households in India have a television set.)

In Pakistan, the number drops to one set per every 73 persons. In Tanzania, it is one per every 297 persons. In Bangladesh, the ratio is one per every 315 persons. In Mozambique, one per every 437 persons.

Then look at countries like Burundi, which has one television set for every 1,175 persons, or Bhutan, which boasts a meager ratio of one television for every 6,180 persons. For the East African country of Rwanda, *Encyclopedia Britannica* lists *no* televisions.

Statistics like these are staggering. Statistics like these are embarrassing if we have been thinking that world evangelization will be done via television.

Compounding these statistics is the fact that in many countries the television station (singular) is government owned and operated, and broadcasting, which is only a few hours a day in most countries, is not allowed to carry any Christian programming.

Does Christian television have its place? Certainly it does. I thank God for Pat Robertson and "The 700 Club," Trinity Broadcasting Network, 100 Huntley Street, and Billy Graham's worldwide telecasts. But we must also realize that the great majority of the people in this generation will never be reached through the medium of television!

Therefore, we cannot adhere to the careless attitude that the world will be won via satellite. It simply will not happen.

In T. L. Osborn's book, *Soulwinning: Out Where The Sinners Are,* he writes:

Let us ever remember this principle: *Sinners won't go to church.* [author's italics] That is the one place they will not go...

We will never win them *inside* [author's italics] the church. We must go out after them—out where the sinners are—as Jesus commanded us to do.

As a whole, sinners do not go to church. And as a whole, sinners throughout the world do not watch Christian television. One reason they will never see a Christian television program is because they will never see a television set!

This is not an attack on television ministries. It is a challenge to open our minds and begin to realize we have been seeing only through American eyes.

This is why I go to huge open fields and public markets and erect a simple wooden platform. It is here that the sinners will come. This is the only place where many will ever hear the Gospel.

We must come face to face with the sin of carelessness that we have harbored and disguised in many ways.

In the heart-stirring book, *Passion for Souls,* by Oswald J. Smith, we read:

> The generally accepted church idea—I mean a little group of believers meeting together on some obscure sheet, struggling to support a pastor, yet *making no impression whatsoever on the multitudes* [author's italics]—is surely not God's vision.

Addressing the issue of the kind of person God uses, T. L. Osborn writes:

> If it can be proven to your satisfaction that healing was for everyone, then you will be expected to pray the prayer of faith, for those who need healing. This will mean that you will need to have a close walk with God.
>
> If our church congregation knew about the empty prayer closets, and lack of personal consecration in the lives of some ministers today, they would be shocked.
>
> Doubtless many who object to the ministry of healing do so because they realize the personal consecration which would automatically be involved if they accepted it.
>
> People can carry on in the circle of normally accepted ministry, and if they possess sufficient talents, they may be praised by their congregations, while in back of the public ministry lies an empty prayer closet, a lack of personal consecration and no days of fasting. They secure their sermons from their loaded

book shelves and their obsolete commentaries, instead of from the altar of their hearts, set aflame by the Holy Ghost.

But the person who stands before an audience of suffering humanity, challenging open combat with satan and his destroying works in humanity, the person who ministers to the sick and who casts out devils, following Christ's example, must be a person of entire consecration to God and full of the Holy Ghost, if they are to be successful.

They are people who fast often and who pray much, because God *only uses people to the extent of their consecration to Him.* [author's italics]

If we expect to be used as a channel of God's power, if we expect our pulpits to grip hearts and change lives, sin must be dealt with, repented of, and put away in our lives. The only obstacle hindering God's power in our lives is—*sin.*

CHAPTER NINETEEN

GREATER WORKS

Most assuredly, I say to you, he who believes in Me, the works that I do he will do also; and greater [works] than these he will do, because I go to My Father.

John 14:12

Wow! This portion of Scripture is potent and power-packed. For most it cannot even be conceived as a promise. It just can't be —it's just too far beyond reason. The religious mind refuses to embrace such a lofty thought. So the pious dismiss it, failing to understand. Unable to organize it, they do nothing.

While Jesus was here He healed the sick, cast out devils, opened blind eyes and deaf ears, caused the lame to walk, calmed the seas, and raised the dead. Entire cites were moved. Some were moved with a sense of awe and expectation as they brought many who were sick and He healed them all. Some were moved with indignation as He offended their religious traditions on the Sabbath, or turned over the tables of the money changers who demeaned the temple of God. No one who encountered Christ remained un-moved. They were either moved to revelation or to a revolution. They either entered into revival or into a riot. Moved they were.

Jesus was fully aware of the realm in which He walked. It was not a dream. He lived it. The world had never before experienced any other who walked in this realm, the realm of God. Jesus knew what He had done and still spoke these words, *"The works that I do shall YOU do also, and even greater works than these..."* There it is in plain English, maybe not easy to understand, but it is there. Jesus said, *"GREATER WORKS!"* Thank God I do not have to understand His ways. Even if my mind cannot organize, under-stand, or comprehend God, His promises, or His ways—I will not put a question mark, where He has put a period. God said it, I believe it, and that settles it!

Something can be greater in magnitude or in number. I choose to believe here that Jesus was speaking of both. Joel 2:28 speaks of God POURING out His Spirit in the last days. These are the last days. God is pouring out His Spirit. Do not think for one moment that if God is POURING out His Spirit, we cannot do the *"greater works"* Jesus spoke of.

The ministry of faith and miracles is indispensable to the evangelization of the world.

What is the prerequisite to doing the *"greater works"*? Jesus said, *"HE WHO BELIEVES."* Religious minds refuse to believe. Cast them down. God did not call you to do what you could afford to do. He did not call you to do what you have the ability to do. He did not call you to do what everyone else is doing. He has called you to greater works! I see no limits or boundaries here. God is too big to be put in your little Pentecostal box. Loose Him and let Him go. Let Him live big in you.

The ministry of faith and miracles is indispensable to the evangelization of the world.

In all of our crusades in foreign countries, people eagerly respond to Jesus with open hearts when they hear the truths of the Gospel and see the power of the Lord manifested in healing the sick.

We have witnessed tens of thousands of Hindus, Muslims, Buddhists, and people of many other religions turn from their dead religions and accept Christ as a direct result of miracles.

Across the body of Christ today, in countries around the world, pastors and laymen are beginning to realize that the supreme task of the Church is the evangelization of the world.

Instead of delegating this mandate of world evangelization to the few missionaries, some are realizing that they can no longer wait on policy-bound organizations to accomplish this supreme task. People are beginning to take the initiative in taking the Gospel to the lost who encompass the globe. Many ears are being opened to the cry of lost humanity who only long for proof of the truth.

These un-evangelized millions do not want theological debates. They will not listen to doctors of divinity. They do not care if you possess the ability to speak to them in their own dialect, and medical missions can never turn their masses to the Gospel.

Men and women with a Pentecostal profession, with no signs and wonders as evidence, can never bring the heathen to Christ with great effectiveness. The un-evangelized demand men and women of faith. They will swarm to hear the one whose message is confirmed with miracles.

Jesus knew exactly what kind of ministry would be required to convince the heathen. With this knowledge, He gave His commission to go to the world with an emphasis on the miraculous. He said:

> Go ye into all the world, and preach the gospel to every creature....
>
> And these signs shall follow them that believe; In my name shall they cast out devils...
>
> ...they shall lay hands on the sick, and they shall recover.
>
> Mark 16:15,17,18

Nothing short of the miracle ministry will ever be effective in bringing the heathen to Christ. The great missionary to the heathen, the apostle Paul, attributed the success of his ministry among the Gentiles to *"...mighty signs and wonders, by the power of the Spirit of God..."* (Romans 15:19).

Without question, a return to Bible methods of evangelism means that we will have Bible results—and millions of heathen souls will be swept into the kingdom of God.

The book of Acts lays the blueprint out for us in our evangelistic efforts: evangelize with signs, wonders, and miracles.

The book of Acts is our example. It must be our pattern for worldwide missionary enterprise. It is our standard for publishing the Gospel. Evangelism and miracles go hand in hand.

Without miracles, evangelism can never succeed. Without evangelism, miracles lose their scriptural objective, which is to convince the heathen or unbeliever of the Gospel.

In the early Church, the divine objective set forth was to preach the Gospel of Christ in every country and to every city with mighty healing miracles to confirm the Church's ministry.

In the Great Commission, Christ combined world evangelism with the ministry of miracles. He made them inseparable, and in accordance with these orders, the early Church acted and produced results.

One man preaching the Gospel today on the mission field with "signs and wonders" following his ministry can win whole tribes to Christ. He can be the means of altering the course and destiny of whole nations.

It has been through the demonstration of God's power in healing the sick, blind, deaf, crippled, and demon-possessed that we have seen hundreds of thousands of souls turn to Christ in more than 90 countries.

There is a worldwide demand for faith and for miracle ministry which must be met. The harvest is ripe. The heathen are waiting. They are waiting to hear men and women who practice the faith they preach. They are waiting for those who prove what they preach by miracles. Jesus has called us to greater works. Take the limits off God!

ENDUEMENT OF POWER

In my book, *A Quest For Souls,* I wrote, "A passion for souls, joined with the power of the Holy Spirit, poses a formidable threat to the kingdom of darkness."

To a small band of believers, anxious to take the Gospel to quench the cry of the lost, Jesus said, *"...tarry in the city of Jerusalem until you are endued with power from on high"* (Luke 24:49).

Heeding the Master's instructions and having been "endued with power from on high," Christ's disciples proceeded to make an unprecedented impact.

> *Great preaching alone is not sufficient to complete the task Christ left for the Church.*

Here is the glory of the Gospel, that in a few years' time, a handful of socially un-influential men, with empty pockets, turned their world upside down (see Acts 17:6).

Great preaching alone is not sufficient to complete the task Christ left for the Church. The clergy today is ever igniting our passion without lighting our paths. Past centuries never produced such a vast array of pulpiteers who could move emotions, expound on Biblical truths, and woo their audiences as have risen forth today.

The founding fathers of the Church, portrayed in the Book of Acts, laid the God-ordained foundations for the fulfillment of the Great Commission.

"Be filled with the Spirit," Paul wrote in Ephesians 5:18. It was the Spirit of God resting upon the heralders of the cross that enabled them to do what no man could accomplish himself.

God considers the anointing of the Holy Spirit of paramount importance. Jesus did not carry on His ministry until the anointing of the Holy Spirit had descended upon Him (see Luke 3:22).

Acts 10:38 states, that *"God anointed Jesus of Nazareth with the Holy Ghost and with power..."*

If we want book of Acts kind of results, we must observe the time-tested, proven ways in which we are to operate.

The great missionary-statesman Oswald J. Smith said in the book, *The Enduement of Power*, *"There is nothing we need so much for our churches and homes, nothing so important for our missionaries and Christian workers, nothing that will count so much in our service for Christ, as the fullness of the Holy Spirit. In fact, God will hold us responsible for the souls we might have won, the work we might have accomplished, had we lived Spirit-filled lives."*

THE SUPREME NEED

Evangelist Charles Finney said, *"Power from on high is the supreme need of the day."*

And F.B. Meyer wrote, *"If Christ waited to be anointed before He went to preach, no young man ought to preach until he, too, has been anointed by the Holy Ghost."*

> *Christ-less sects are on a worldwide rampage to persuade millions.*

Christ-less sects are on a world-wide rampage to persuade millions. They are deluging this generation with thousands of tons of their literature. While wholesale persuasion of non-Christian religions is taking place, many churches are counterproductive in their efforts, because they do not rely on the miracle energy of the Holy Spirit.

"Ye shall receive power, after that the Holy Ghost is come upon you: and ye shall be witnesses unto me," Jesus said in Acts 1:8.

Paul wrote, *"My speech and my preaching was not with enticing words of man's wisdom, but in demonstration of the Spirit and of power"* (1 Corinthians 24).

Luke reported, *"...they were all filled with the Holy Ghost, and they spake the word of God with boldness... Now when they saw the boldness of Peter and John, and perceived that they were unlearned and ignorant men, they marvelled..."* (Acts 4:31,13).

The Word of God is very explicit concerning this unique gift of the baptism of the Holy Spirit. It is not an option to be bypassed. It was not given for the sole purpose of speaking in tongues. Most people have made tongues the goal in this experience. Once it is attained, they settle down to a fruitless Christian life.

World evangelism is every Christian's ministry. The purpose of being filled with the Holy Spirit is not to speak in tongues, but to give proof of the resurrection—to boldly witness Christ in the power of the Spirit.

The significance of a Spirit-filled life is that we will no longer be a "reproach among the heathen." God has empowered and equipped us so we shall be able to reap our inheritance of the souls in our generation.

In his soul-stirring book, *Sodom Had No Bible,* Leonard Ravenhill says, *"There is but one way to save this generation. It is the way of the Christ, and the outpouring of the Holy Ghost."*

The apostle Paul saw the passion of his Lord, the power of the Gospel, and the possibilities of Pentecost. Nothing less could suffice.

THE PURPOSE OF PENTECOST: POWER!

Pentecost in Bible times had a purpose. The Pentecostal experience today also has a purpose. The purpose is namely this—power!

First, it is power over sin. The Bible says, *"Walk in the Spirit, and you shall not fulfill the lust of the flesh"* (Galatians 5:16). Without the fullness of the Holy Spirit, we have no choice but to be a slave to sin. Power to live a victorious Christian life is a vital benefit of the Spirit-filled life.

Second, it is power in service: *"Ye shall receive power, after that the Holy Ghost is come upon you: and ye shall be witnesses unto me"* (Acts 1:8).

It is the energizing power of the Spirit-filled believer, nothing else, that compounds the effectiveness of all his efforts. Without a realization of the Spirit's infilling, we can only work in the energy of the flesh instead of the power of the spirit.

This is the purpose of the fullness of the Spirit—power! Power over sin and power in service.

The Spirit-filled life will impose a new threat to the forces of hell. Conviction will grip the hearts of those to whom you preach or witness.

EVIDENCE OF THE SPIRIT-FILLED LIFE

Clearly defined throughout the Scriptures is that power is the evidence of the Spirit-filled life.

What was the evidence to Elisha that he had received a double portion of Elijah's spirit? It was summed up in the fact that Elisha now had Elijah's power, so when he, too, smote the waters of the Jordan with Elijah's mantle, they divided the same as they had for Elijah.

...unless I have power over sin and power in service, I am not living the fullness of the Spirit.

I must belabor the fact that unless I have power over sin and power in service, I am not living the fullness of the Spirit. Power alone is the evidence that one has been baptized in the Holy Spirit.

THE SPIRIT DESCENDS ON JESUS

Jesus Himself was baptized in the Spirit. John said in Mark 1:8:

> I indeed baptized you with water, but He (Jesus) will baptize you with the Holy Spirit.

The passage continues:

> It came to pass in those days that Jesus came from Nazareth of Galilee, and was baptized by John in the Jordan.

> And immediately, coming up from the water, He saw the heavens parting and the Spirit descending upon Him like a dove.

> Mark 1:9-10

Jesus told His disciples that they were to *"tarry in the city of Jerusalem until they were endued with power from on high"* (Luke 24:49). And in Ephesians 5:18 believers are commanded to be filled with the Spirit.

This precedent has been established from the foundation of the early Church. It is not to be judged and analyzed; rather, it is to be believed and obeyed!

In Acts 1:4–5, the disciples are told not to depart from Jerusalem, but *"...wait for the Promise of the Father... you shall be baptized with the Holy Spirit not many days from now."*

Yes, Jesus did say to *"tarry until,"* but that was before the Day of Pentecost. God's appointed time for the sending of the Spirit was the Day of Pentecost. Luke records in Acts 2:1, *"And when the day of Pentecost was fully come..."*

THE TIME IS AT HAND

The disciples were ready, but the Spirit had never, to that point, been given. After Pentecost, no waiting was necessary. Cornelius and his house did not tarry; they received at once.

The Samaritan Christians knew nothing of tarrying. They received as rapidly as Peter and John prayed.

Paul's converts at Ephesus did not wait. Paul laid his hands on them and at once the Spirit was given. And so it has always been given since the Day of Pentecost.

WHAT IS "PENTECOST"?

"Pentecost" is not a denomination. The word refers to the feast day on which the early Christians were first filled with the Holy Spirit.

Vast multitudes of Christians have received the experience of being filled with the Holy Spirit, but because many mainline denominations officially opposed speaking in tongues, Pentecostal denominations were formed.

The regrettable result was that people began to confuse being filled with the Holy Spirit with Pentecostal church doctrines.

The baptism of the Holy Spirit is an enduement of power available to all believers. To the critics of this experience I would say, if there are degrees in death, then the deadest I know is to preach about the Holy Spirit *without* the anointing of the Holy Spirit!

> *The baptism of the Holy Spirit is an enduement of power available to all believers.*

The world is clamoring to know the truth. Christ deemed it necessary to be filled with the Spirit before beginning His earthly ministry. He also saw the necessity of being *"endued with power from on high"* for the work into which He launched His disciples.

Nothing less than the anointing of the Holy Spirit was sufficient for the man of God then, and the same holds true for us today. The baptism of the Holy Spirit is the order for the day. It is the greatest need of the hour.

Five billion people need to see the truth of the Gospel in demonstration and power. Only the infilling of the Spirit will bring that reality to humanity.

My convictions about being filled with the Holy Spirit may seem ambiguous to some and controversial to others, but they have evolved from the platforms of a worldwide soul-winning ministry where what I have said about Christ has had to be (and is) demonstrated. *That is the purpose of Pentecost.*

Armed with His Word, endued with His power, commissioned by His Spirit, it is time to go forth! We have been chosen for *greater* works!

If you have not yet been filled, ask and receive today (see Luke 11:9–13).

CHAPTER TWENTY

THEY SHALL SHARE ALIKE

How then shall they call on Him in whom they have believed? And how shall they believe in Him of whom they have not heard? And how shall they hear without a preacher? And how shall they preach unless they are sent?

Romans 10:14–15

These are relatively simple questions posed here in this passage. There is a very simple answer to each—they CANNOT. One cannot hear and believe without a preacher to proclaim the Gospel message. A preacher cannot go, unless he is sent. This fact makes the "senders" and those who "go," each of equal importance. Without the senders, the preachers are left at home in silence. Without those who would go, the senders would have no voice. Those who go give legs to those who have the financial resources, and the desire to spread the Gospel message.

The Bible tells us: *"There are many members, yet one body"* (I Cor. 12:20). It is the body of Christ coming together, each one bringing their gifts and talents, for the furtherance of the Kingdom of God. People have different callings and anointings, yet it is God who gives the increase. (I Cor. 3:7)

I planted, Apollos watered, but God gave the
increase. So then neither he who plants is anything,
nor he who waters, but God who gives the increase.
Now he who plants and he who waters are one, and
each one will receive his own reward according to
his own labor. For we are God's fellow workers...

I Corinthians 3:6-9

DIFFERENT GIFTS

I believe many ministers have done a great injustice to a certain
segment of the body of Christ. If a successful businessman comes to
a church, he carries himself in a way that speaks of confidence.
These men have been gifted in areas many have not. The standard
operating procedure of these financially successful men and women
seems to be this: Remove him from his arena of expertise, strip him
of his success, and send them off into Bible school/ministry

The Church creates a subtle pressure to make a minister out of
every member. Some do carry the call of God upon their lives and
they should enter into the pulpit ministry. But some of those same
people have a different gift and call; they have been called into
the office of a king. While each gift and call is different, each is of
equal importance.

And has made us kings and priests to His God and
Father, to Him [be] glory and dominion forever and
ever. Amen.

Revelation 1:6

In the Bible the role of the priests was to hear from God, receive tithes and offerings, care for the house of God, widows and orphans, and to encourage the people before battle.

The role of the king was to destroy the enemies of God, take the spoils of war, govern the natural affairs of the nation, and to give tithes and offerings to the priests.

In his book, *Kings & Priests* David High writes: *"The priests see that a harvest of souls is coming and they want to build buildings, hire staff, print training materials, etc. Because the king's side of the kingdom is underdeveloped, the priests start talking more about what is missing (the provision) than they do about the vision.*

> # The role of the king was to destroy the enemies of God...

Today, we have churches full of frustrated kings sitting in pews with their arms folded listening to frustrated priests who have heard from God, but don't have the money to make it happen.

When priests, in their instruction to the Church, include the king's office as an option of legitimate God consecrated service and men see that office clearly, the kingdom of God on earth will go through a radical transformation."

David High goes on to say, "Kings, who have all this love for God and drive to produce wealth yet have no heaven authorized vision, will sometimes create a vision of their own and hope that they can somehow get God to bless it."

Many who have been called, and anointed, to finance the Gospel live in a frustrated state. The two different offices of a king and a priest should complement, not compete with each other. The call to PROVISION is just as important as the minister who receives the VISION.

> But as his part [is] who goes down to the battle, so [shall] his part [be] who stays by the supplies; they shall share alike.
>
> I Samuel 30:24

If God has called you to be a "sender," then treasure what He has entrusted to you. The world is waiting for the manifestation of your gift—You can touch eternity.

CHAPTER TWENTY-ONE

IT'S JUST THE BEGINNING

Critics offer plenty of pessimistic thoughts when a dream from God is unveiled. Whether they are intimidated, embarrassed, or

Don't share your 16x20 dreams with 3x5 minds.

just love to be compliant to the "status quo," we don't truly know their reasons for their bleak outlook concerning the dream. What we do know is that opposition to a dream is easily found. One does not have to look far to see an army of the narrow-minded being

assembled. It is easy to join the ranks of the "Dr. Do Little's." The "Mr. Do Nothing's" welcome members by the thousands. Don't share your 16x20 dreams with 3x5 minds.

In 1993, I was awarded an honorary doctorate. This was bestowed upon me based "in view of my accomplishments in world evangelism." This university had taken inventory of our efforts and successes and decided they had merit in their decision in granting me the doctorate.

Although I have never really used the title of "Dr.," some had challenged the validity of this honorary degree. As the critics pursue academic years in the classroom, they demean the "honorary" portion of the degree. I have an earned doctorate, and an honorary one. I received the later for DOING the things that those in the classroom merely study and talk about doing. It is not what you know; it's what you do. A head full of knowledge goes to the grave as wasted grey matter, unless this knowledge is used in action—to produce fruit.

FOUNDATION FOR THE FUTURE

The book of Acts is no history book. Treating it as such will reduce this blueprint for success in ministry, to a mere relic, void of power. It is not a history book. It is HIS-STORY. The revealed power of the book of Acts is that God is still writing HIS-STORY in the world today.

> **The former account I made, O Theophilus, of all that Jesus began both to do and teach,**
>
> **Acts 1:1**

The Gospels are record of the works of Christ while He was here in His earthly ministry. The book of Acts is a record of the beginning works of Christ through His church. Note this—it is just the beginning!

I want to bring your attention to the last chapter and the last verse of the Epistles.

> **To God, alone wise, be glory through Jesus Christ forever. Amen.**
>
> **Romans 16:27**

The grace of our Lord Jesus Christ be with you.

> 1 Corinthians 16:23

My love be with you all in Christ Jesus. Amen.

> 1 Corinthians 16:24

The grace of the Lord Jesus Christ, and the love of God, and the communion of the Holy Spirit be with you all. Amen.

> 2 Corinthians 13:14

Brethren, the grace of our Lord Jesus Christ be with your spirit. Amen.

> Galatians 6:18

Grace be with all those who love our Lord Jesus Christ in sincerity. Amen.

> Ephesians 6:24

The grace of our Lord Jesus Christ be with you all. Amen.

> Philippians 4:23

This salutation by my own hand—Paul. Remember my chains. Grace be with you. Amen.

> Colossians 4:18

The grace of our Lord Jesus Christ be with you. Amen.

1 Thessalonians 5:28

Continue to read the Epistles and you will find that each one has a conclusion. "Grace be with you all. Amen." The book is finished.

Now I want to turn your attention to the final chapter of the book of Acts. Let us read the last two written verses of this book:

> **Then Paul dwelt two whole years in his own rented house, and received all who came to him, preaching the kingdom of God and teaching the things which concern the Lord Jesus Christ with all confidence, no one forbidding him.**

Acts 28:30-31

There is NO *"grace be with you all, amen,"* here. No benediction, no salutation. WHY? Because God is not finished writing the book of Acts! In this generation, God is

God is not finished writing the book of Acts!

writing another chapter to the book of Acts. In my life, I have determined to write another chapter to the book of Acts. People look with an awe at the works of Christ's disciples that are recorded in Acts. Yet, we possess everything that Paul, Peter, and Philip possessed, and MORE. *Technology alone dictates and demands that we surpass and exceed the accomplishments of the early Church!* How big is YOUR God? How much is too much?

I have heard Christians around the world make comments like this: "When I get to heaven I want to sit next to Moses and hear how he led three million people out of captivity." "When I get to heaven I want to sit next to Elijah and hear about the miracles he witnessed." "When I get to heaven I want to sit next to Peter, or Paul, or John and hear of their great exploits."

I say, why don't you do enough on this earth so that when you get to heaven, Moses, Elijah, Peter, and Paul want to sit next to you?

Who has decreed that Biblical miracles and exploits were to be the pinnacle of success? Did Jesus not say that we would do even great works than He? (See John 14:12). *History is not a divine force set in stone; it is the servant of those who make it.* This liberating idea makes room for us to dream once again. Stale methods and ideologies have always given way to the "dreamers" of their day.

> *Faith says, "I can live out of my imagination, instead of my memory."*

Faith says, "I can live out of my imagination, instead of my memory. I can tie myself to my limitless potential, instead of my limiting past." As one songwriter puts it, "Let your faith do the talking." Vision replaces mental resistance.

In my book, *Vision, Passion, And The Pursuit of God* I wrote:

"The movers and shakers who shape our world all possess a common quality that catapults them ahead of the crowd on their way to achieving their accolades. Each possesses an inalienable burning passion to attain their visionary ideas."

Driven, excessive, narrow-minded, and consumed are adjectives describing these firebrands. But it is the man with a vision, touched by the fire of God, and consumed with a passion to fulfill the vision who will always bear the brunt of the critic's tongue. The only limitations we have are the size of our dreams and the degree of our determination. Who is the man who can determine what is impossible? For the dreams of yesterday are the hope of today—the reality of our tomorrow. Every great achievement commanding honor in the annals of the world, began as a dream. Nothing great was ever achieved without it.

> *I have determined to use my life to write another chapter to the book of Acts.*

For twenty-five years, we have been privileged to lead millions of people to the foot of the Cross. We have built nearly 700 churches, given away 83 mobile evangelism units, and sowed more than 2 million books into the nations of the world. It is just the beginning! I am on a world-wide quest to win 100 million people to Christ. I will build at least 1,000 churches. I will provide mobile evangelism units to at least 100 nations. I will continue to sow millions of books into the nations of the world. I have determined to use my life to write another chapter to the book of Acts.

CHAPTER TWENTY-TWO

ABSOLUTE POWER

I once asked R.W. Shambach what he thought was the greatest key to success in ministry. I prefaced the question by stating that I was aware of the many factors that play a role in achieving successful ministry, but I wanted to know what he thought was the greatest key to success in ministry. Without hesitation he said, *"Just go, two thirds of God is GO!"* I posed that very same question to T.L. Osborn. This man of God has probably influenced and impacted more people in this world than anyone in the history of mankind. I said, "T.L., what would you say is the greatest key to success in ministry?" He responded, *"Just care for people."* That simple, yet that powerful. Several years ago I asked Lester Sumrall that very same question. He was quick to respond with what he determined to be the great key to ministerial success. Brother Sumrall's response, *"Just don't, quit!"* Someone once asked me what I thought was the greatest key to success in ministry. My response, *"Just go, care for people, and don't quit!"*

Several minutes after T.L. Osborn's initial response to my question, he continued with two more powerful points. He said, *"I suppose the second part of the answer to that question would be this—having enough faith in what you believe that when you seed people with it, it will change their lives, and then just go and do it."* Then he also said to me, *"SEED is absolute power because it must produce exactly what it is."*

We see the Scriptural foundation of this truth in the book of Genesis.

> God said, "Let the earth bring forth grass, the herb that yields seed, and the fruit tree that yield fruit according to its kind, whose seed is in itself on the earth;" and it was so.
>
> **Genesis 1:11**

There are natural laws and spiritual laws that govern the affairs of man in this earth. Just as there is a law of gravity that keeps our feet firmly on the ground, there is a law concerning the seed which dictates it must produce ACCORDING TO IT'S OWN KIND. An apple seed has no ability to grow anything other than an apple tree. An orange seed will never produce a harvest of rice. No, the law of Genesis chapter one says seed must produce according to it's own kind. This makes seed absolute power, because it MUST produce exactly what it is!

Then He taught them many things by parables, and said to them in His teaching:

> Listen! Behold a sower went out to sow. And it happened, as he sowed, that some seed fell by the wayside; and the birds of the air came and devoured it. Some fell on stony ground, where it did not have much earth; and immediately it sprang up because it had no depth of earth. But when the sun was up it was scorched, and because it had no root it withered away. And some seed fell among thorns; and the thorns grew up and choked it, and it yielded

no crop. But other seed fell on good ground and yielded a crop that sprang up, increased and produced: some thirtyfold, some sixty, and some a hundred...THE SOWER SOWS THE WORD.

Mark 4:2-8,14

And He said; "The Kingdom of God is as if a man should scatter seed on the ground, and should sleep by night and rise by day, and the seed should sprout and grow, he himself does not know how. For the earth yields crops by itself: first the blade, then the head, after that the full grain ripens, immediately he puts in the sickle because the harvest has come."

Mark 4:26-29

In Mark 4:30, we read of the parable of the mustard seed and the potency and potential proclaimed here. The entire fourth chapter of Mark brings us an array of parables that deal specifically with "seed." In Matthew 13:38, Jesus said: *"The field is the world."*

Preachers today have fashioned themselves after predecessors who have developed their own unique style. They have been taught how to hold an audience in rapt attention. Their command of the English language and skill in their delivery are unequaled. The emotions can be turned on and off; some can command a well timed and executed tear that brings a sense of awe to the listeners and touches their emotions moving them to respond.

I believe one simple fact remains, God uses us in spite of ourselves. Some are more polished than others. Some have a stronger anointing than others. In truth, we're all farmers in the Kingdom of God. Jesus said, *"The SOWER sows the WORD."* His anointing rests on His Word. His power is revealed through His Word. His Word is seed and that seed must produce exactly what it is.

> I planted, Apollos watered, but God gave the increase... Now he who plants and he who waters are one, and each will receive his own reward according to his own labor. For we are God's fellow workers, you are God's field.
>
> 1 Corinthians 3:6,8-9

We are not required to produce the results, only to sow the seed.

It is God who gives the increase. As mortal beings, we have no ability to save or heal another person, but the seed we deliver has absolute ability to do so. This relieves us of pressure to "make it happen," for we cannot. We are not required to produce the results, only to sow the seed.

THE FOLLY OF THE WHEAT FARMER

Let's say there is a man who year after year always produces an abundant crop when harvest time dawns. He is the best "sower" in the land. He could conduct seminars on sowing techniques and teach about wheat farming. He could even give a demonstration how to sow the seed, and bring back the results to the class a few months later to show the harvest. The grateful students could remark on what a great wheat farmer he is. Forget it.

It is not due to special techniques of the sower, but rather it is because of the inherent value and power of the seed itself.

THE POWER IS IN THE SEED. If a wheat seed is sown, it must produce a wheat harvest.

It is not due to special techniques of the sower, but rather it is because of the inherent value and power of the seed itself. Jesus slotted us in the category of farmers. He said the sower sows the seed, and the seed is the word of God. The law of the seed demands that it must produce exactly what it is.

> Having been born again, not of corruptible SEED but incorruptible, through the WORD OF GOD which LIVES and abides forever... The Word of the Lord endures forever.
>
> I Peter 1:23–25

> For the Word of God is LIVING and powerful, and sharper than any two edged sword...
>
> Hebrews 4:12

Only the "imperishable seed" can bring about imperishable results. The Bible says, *"Every seed brings forth after its own kind."* Each promise, by the blessing promised, reveals the nature of the harvest of promises fulfilled. All of God's wonderful works are potentially in the seed.

A healing seed will produce a healing harvest. A seed of salvation brings new life to a fertile heart. God's Word is LIFE and that word sown into the soil of a person's heart will produce LIFE. The Word is Life, and it is powerful. It must produce the very life of God where it is sown.

I remember a crusade we conducted in Hubli, India. It was a powerful meeting as more than 100,000 packed the field. One night a little eight year old girl was brought up to testify. For several years, this precious child was completely blind as thick cataracts covered her eyes. As she stood on the platform with her mother, it was an extremely emotional time for the Indian family. The little girl could see for the first time in years.

It was a tremendous miracle. The multitude stood amazed. A number of those people looked at me with a sense of awe. They thought I had a special faith that brought the wonderful miracle. Forget about it. Don't blame me for that miracle; I did not even know she was there. It was the Word, the Seed, the Life, that was manifested in her young life. Seed is absolute power because it must produce what it is. It was the seed that produced life in the eyes where there was no life.

T.L. Osborn passed on a truth to me that F.F. Bosworth related to him. He said: *"If it is worth preaching it is worth recording. If it is worth recording, it is worth putting into a book. The Truth is the same whether it is spoken or written."* It is the power of the seed.

Jesus said to them, "My food is to do the will of Him who sent Me, and to finish His work. Do you not say, There are still four months and then comes the harvest? Behold I say to you, lift up your eyes and look at the fields, for they are already white for harvest! And he who reaps receives wages, and gathers fruit for eternal life, that both he who SOWS and he who reaps may rejoice together. For in this the saying is true: one sows and another reaps. I sent you to reap that for which you have not labored; others have labored, and you have entered into their labors."

John 4:34-38

In our international crusades, we have experienced times when we have entered into the labors of others, and reaped an amazing harvest. Madagascar, Liberia, Thailand, and many others proved to be fantastic harvests of souls. In other places, we conducted the same type of miracle crusade, but it was a time of sowing and watering. All we can really do is sow the Word, and that is all we are instructed to do. It is God, and God alone, who gives the increase and harvest. The sower sows the Word. Seed is absolute power. God gives the increase.

SEED IS POWERLESS UNTIL IT IS PLANTED. NOTHING CAN TAKE THE PLACE OF SEED, NOT EVEN PRAYER!

He who observes the wind will not sow, and he who regards the clouds will not reap. As you do not know what is the way of the wind, or how the bones grow in the womb of her who is with child, so you do not know the works of God who makes everything,

In the morning sow your seed, and in the evening do
not withhold your hand; for you do not know which
will prosper, Either this or that, or whether both
alike will be good.

Ecclesiastes 11:4–6

People want to pray the power down. You preach the power
out. Seed is absolute power, it must produce exactly what it is. The
sower sows the Word.

So shall My Word be that goes forth from My mouth;
It shall not return to Me void, But it shall accomplish
what I please, And it shall prosper in the thing for
which I sent it.

Isaiah 55:11

Speak the Word faithfully (Jer. 23:28), speak the Word boldly
(Acts 4:29), preach the Word (Acts 8:25), and do the Word
(James 1:22).

SEED IS ABSOLUTE POWER!

In the seed are infinite possibilities. In F.F. Bosworth's timeless masterpiece, *Christ the Healer,* he says, *"One verse of scripture allowed to germinate in a human heart may grow into a harvest of thousands of conversions and the* 'eternal glory' which follows. The justice of God requires that He make the seed grow when it is 'planted' and 'watered.'"

The sower sows the seed. The seed is the Word.

Nothing can take the place of seed, and that seed remains powerless until it is planted. SEED IS ABSOLUTE POWER! It will produce life.

CHAPTER TWENTY-THREE

EN MASSE
(WHY I BELIEVE IN MASS CRUSADE EVANGELISM)

Words fail to describe an international crusade. There is a crude wooden platform, a huge open field, and a sea of humanity packed so tight, no one can move. The needs of these people span an incredible range. Their search for truth stands unparalleled.

My eyes have beheld His wonders and glory as the Gospel was presented in simplicity, yet demonstrated with great power. As miracles manifest outside the sanctuary, this most unlikely place becomes a haven for the Most High. In these crusades, I have seen the lepers cleansed and the cripples walk. Blind eyes have opened and the deaf have heard. The miracles abound regardless of race, age, sex, or religion. God is at hand. The miracles speak volumes.

We are involved with many avenues of ministry around the world, but I am first and foremost a crusader. I have dedicated my life to mass evangelism. There is nothing like giving an altar call for those who would give their lives to Christ after seeing numerous miracles take place before their eyes. I have witnessed more than 300,000 people respond and accept Jesus at one time. There have been millions more around the world. For years all they had known was religion. Now, Truth greeted them for the first time in their lives. It is not a difficult decision once they see Truth demonstrated.

For years, I have heard the critics' narrow minded opinions concerning mass evangelism. "You are committing spiritual abortion, 'God said to go and make disciples, not converts', and 'What about follow-up?'"

I have come to realize that much of this criticism is based on jealousy. Those who seem to be most vocal with their demeaning words are the ones who cannot get a crowd themselves. Ignorance provides the basis for their objections to mass crusade evangelism.

Thus, this is my purpose in penning this chapter. We must not discount a medium of ministry just because we do not truly under-stand it. In this chapter I will address the questions and objections. We will go to the Word, particularly the book of Acts, and discover the master blueprint for success. Here I will show you why I believe in mass crusade evangelism.

At this very moment I am in Peru, and we have just finished our Arequipa crusade. The pastors and people are astounded by what has taken place. For many of those who were there, they witnessed miracles for the very first time. Everything that has transpired during the past five days has made an impact upon their lives, and a lasting impression upon their minds. An air of excitement and expectation has already spread throughout the city. Thousands have accepted Christ. To experience such an event would quickly make you a believer in mass crusade evangelism.

Let me begin by addressing a few of the critics' objections that have been passed down over the years. Here are a few of the most widely acclaimed negative attitudes towards mass crusade evangelism:

1. You are committing "spiritual abortion."

I am not completely sure about the actual meaning of this viewpoint, but I believe the attitude is one of concern for the brand new convert.

First, let me begin by saying, I absolutely believe in follow-up. We have printed hundreds of thousands of Bibles and follow-up packets. We give them away by the tons. We have taken the names and addresses of scores of these new converts and given them to local pastors. We have planted churches and built church buildings that have been filled to capacity following a crusade. We have held numerous new convert classes following our crusades. I believe in follow-up. One must realize, however, there must be an "up" before you can ever have a "follow-up." The conversion of a lost soul is the very first step.

I remember our Nellore, India crusade which we held a number of years ago. It was a tremendous success. We struggled with finances to purchase 15,000 Bibles and books for the converts of this crusade. It was a joy to give those, however we recorded 37,000 decisions for Christ during this five day campaign. A couple from the United States traveled with me and wept as they observed the phenomenal miracles and mass salvations. Upon their return to the U.S., their voices were ones of criticism. Why? They said it was wrong for us to provide such a limited amount of follow-up material. They said there were 22,000 new converts who did not receive any books, or Bible. They said those new converts may enjoy heaven one day, but they will probably live a defeated life here on this earth.

Given the finances, I would have gladly provided the funds for Bibles and books for the rest of the converts. I had exhausted all the resources I had at that time. In addition to this, I would rather see someone live a defeated life on this earth and still partake of eternal glory than just say, "We will not tell you the good news for no one is here to provide proper follow-up."

God knows how to take care of His own.

We have no right to negate the work of the Holy Spirit in the life of a child of God. I truly believe God knows how to take care of His own. To the believers at Ephesus Paul wrote: *"So now, brethren, I commend you to God and to the word of His grace, which is able to build you up and give you an inheritance among all those who are sanctified."*

Being confident of this very thing, that He who has begun a good work in you will complete it until the day of Jesus Christ.

Philippians 1:6

My dear friend, Pastor Surapong in Chiangrai Thailand, told me a wonderful story of God's mercy. He said a man arrived in his church one day seeking a new church home as they had just relocated to Chiangrai. As he spoke to Pastor Surapong, he told him how six months earlier he had accepted Christ in a miracle crusade. He said that all his life he had been a Buddhist, but upon attending this crusade his crippled arm was healed, leading to his salvation. Then he said, "You know, you look a lot like the man who interpreted for the American preacher in that meeting." He was! It was during our first crusade in Thailand that this man received his miracle and accepted Christ. Some three hundred miles separated the two cities. There was no follow-up on this particular man by us, but the miracle of new birth in his life caused him to seek out a church long after the crusade was over.

I am fully persuaded that the work of the Holy Spirit in the life of a child of God far surpasses our expectations. I believe that the gift of salvation is a far greater sustaining grace than all our effort of follow-up could ever produce. I am convinced that the parable of the shepherd who left the ninety-nine to find the one lost sheep speaks volumes of God's follow-up program. We

> *I believe that the gift of salvation is a far greater sustaining grace than all our effort of follow-up could ever produce.*

must do all within our power to assure a strong walk with the Lord for those we bring to the foot of the Cross. We must realize His grace supercedes all else.

2. The Word of God instructs us to make disciples, not converts.

To those who have questioned the effectiveness of mass evangelism in the making of disciples, I would point your attention to the eleventh chapter of the Book of Acts.

Here, revival had broken out. A great number of people (masses, in fact) had just turned to the Lord. What was the response of the Church? Did they criticize their methods or numbers? How did they respond to this great influx of new believers?

> And the hand of the Lord was with them, and a great
> number believed and turned to the Lord.
> Then news of these things came to the ears of the
> church in Jerusalem, and they sent out Barnabas to
> go as far as Antioch.
> When he came and had seen the grace of God, he
> was glad, and encouraged them all that with pur-
> pose of heart they should continue with the Lord.
> For he was a good man, full of the Holy Spirit and of
> faith.And a great many people were added to the Lord.
> Then Barnabas departed for Tarsus to seek Saul.
> And when he had found him, he brought him to
> Antioch. So it was that for a whole year they assembled
> with the church and taught a great many people.And
> the disciples were first called Christians in Antioch.
>
> Acts 11:21–26

The news of God's outpouring reached the church, and THEY SENT ministers to continue with the disciple-making process.

Again in Acts 8, we see the pattern of the early church develop further.

Then Philip went down to the city of Samaria and preached Christ to them.

And the multitudes with one accord heeded the things spoken by Philip, hearing and seeing the miracles which he did…

Now when the apostles who were at Jerusalem heard that Samaria had received the word of God, they sent Peter and John to them, who when they had come down, prayed for them that they might receive the Holy Spirit.

Acts 8:5-6,14-15

The Bible clearly states that it is the whole body fitly joined together. Each has his part, each a role to fulfill. Philip won the multitude to Christ, then THEY (the church) SENT. No one person has ever had the mandate to fulfill each and every aspect of ministry—each one must work together in the process.

In Acts 8:26–40, the Spirit of the Lord led Philip to bring the Gospel message to the Ethiopian eunuch. Salvation came and Philip was whisked away just as abruptly as he appeared. Why did God not leave him there to train and instruct this "new creation?" What stance did God take in regards to the Ethiopian soul? *"My grace is sufficient for thee"* (II Cor. 12:9) is spoken by the mere fact God took him away. Yes, do all you can to disciple the new convert, but God is bigger than our plans.

In Mark chapter five, it depicts the powerful story of the deliverance of the Gadarene demoniac. As Jesus met him in the tombs, the devils were expelled. Freedom and peace flooded his soul.

Salvation met him at his dire time of need. Moments later, the "Gadarene Demoniac was clothed and in his right mind."

Did Jesus immediately enroll him in His disciple making program? Did He take him under His wing and tutor the young man? Although the man begged Jesus that he might follow Him and be with Him (Mark 5:18) Jesus did not permit him. Instead, he sent him out into his own ministry, just hours after coming to know the Savior.

> However, Jesus did not permit him, but said to him, "Go (the mission and commission) home to your friends, and tell (the mandate) them what great things the Lord has done for you (the message), and how He has had compassion (the motive—love) on you. And he departed and began to proclaim in Decapolis (the multitude, ten cities) all that Jesus had done for him; and all marveled (the miracle)."
>
> Mark 5:19–20

3. God is not into numbers.

The sheer size of the crowds that gather during a mass crusade draws criticism, usually from those who want a crowd but cannot get one. Yes, Jesus did take the time for the one woman at the well. He quieted the rebukes of His disciples as they scorned the blind man who cried out for mercy, then went and ministered to him. Yet, we see numerous accounts through the Gospels of the mass meetings He conducted.

Roof tearing faith was demonstrated by the paralytic as he made his own dramatic entrance into the presence of Jesus. Why? Because of the multitudes who filled the house. When the woman with the issue of blood finally reached the place where Jesus was, she suddenly realized she was not alone. The Bible says a MULTITUDE of people were thronging Jesus. The Gospel depicts a Jesus who was moved with compassion because of the MULTITUDES (Matthew 9:36).

How many did Moses lead out of captivity? How many did Jesus feed with the five loaves and two small fishes? How many did Peter speak to on the day of Pentecost?

> **The MULTITUDES with one accord heeded the things spoken by Philip, hearing and seeing the miracles which he did.**
>
> Acts 8:6

"God is not into numbers." That is not what I see when I read my Bible. Jesus did not neglect the single woman at the well, nor did he get excited about the multitudes. Yet much of his time was spent ministering to the masses.

CRUSADE BENEFITS

Obviously, the most important factor in mass crusade evangelism is the conversion of great multitudes. Our miracle crusades draw from 10,000 to more than 300,000 people a night. Miracles that take place during the crusade cause the crowds to explode in attendance. The sheer size of the crowds draws a great deal of attention in the media. Usually, the city takes notice.

Conducting such events in stadiums, parks, market places, and huge open fields is non-threatening to the unsaved. Those of other religious persuasions feel a certain sense of comfortability in these neutral venues. This leads to huge numbers of the un-churched who attend the meetings. Thus, the salvation message spans a large sector of the city, those who would never attend a church meeting often come to these crusade services.

Another powerful plus of mass evangelism in a targeted city is the new credibility the local churches experience. In our crusades, we work very closely with the local churches in that city. Their high profile position on the platform and with the crusade identifies them with our team and ministry. The city looks at them with a whole new respect. The huge crowds and undeniable miracles grant the churches a credibility that previously had eluded them. Within the churches themselves, a crusade brings a whole new level of unity among the pastors and churches.

> *...a crusade brings a whole new level of unity among the pastors and churches.*

Evangelistic efforts void of demonstration and the power of God suffer severe limits in their effectiveness in dark and lost lands. A miracle settles the issue for those who question the Gospel message. When the blind see and lame walk, Truth is demonstrated. As the unbelievers witness the powerful testimonies, they whole-heartedly turn to Christ by the thousands. People seek Truth. Truth is easily embraced when it is proven.

> Our children too shall serve him, for they shall hear
> from us about the wonders of the Lord; generations
> yet unborn shall hear of all the miracles he did for us.
>
> Psalms 22:30,31 (TLB)

The power of the miracles reach far beyond the crusade site. MIRACLES PREACH FOR GENERATIONS TO COME. The signs and wonders are powerful convincers during crusade days, yet they do not lose their affect after the platforms have been disassembled. When the recipients of the heavenly gifts go home, so do their testimonies. For days, weeks, months, and years to come their stories are repeated time and again. The Gospel story spreads. The love of Christ contends for the hearts of man.

MIRACLES PREACH FOR GENERATIONS TO COME.

I was in the nation of Tanzania conducting a large open-air campaign. One night, an old Muslim woman attended the meeting. For thirty years she had been bowed over. For three months she had not even left her mud hut. Early that day she crawled on her hands and knees down the mountain side. It took her all day to finally get to the stadium, but she made it.

That night she received her miracle. For the first time in three months she stood up, then for the first time in THIRTY YEARS she stood up straight. The vast audience cheered as she walked, totally healed, across the platform. After the meeting was over, one of the pastors accompanied her home. He later told me that as she walked to her house that night the old woman's neighbors began to cheer. "Look at momma, momma got healed, momma got her miracle!" they cheered.

Those people never attended the crusade, but they were still presented with the Gospel. Miracles preach for generations to come. Miracles preach to those who never attend a church service. Crusade evangelism creates a neutral ground where sinners can feel welcome, and a place for the miracle power of God to be manifested.

Our Guinea, West Africa crusade produced a powerful miracle that preached to a Muslim government. On the final day of the Conakry crusade, a prominent politician brought his twelve year old deaf and dumb son to the crusade. A marvelous miracle transpired and the young boy spoke and heard for the first time in his life. It was reported the next day that the politician proclaimed the "good news" throughout parliament. A miracle preaches for generations to come.

Vision is birthed in the hearts of those most connected with the crusade. The event eclipsed all they ever imagined possible. A spirit of evangelism permeates the hearts of the hungry. New potential is released. Vision of a Great God is caught. Nothing is impossible.

Vision is birthed in the hearts of those most connected with the crusade.

The success, size, and miracles at a mass miracle crusade gives us a voice in the city that we could never have without it. In the

Arequipa, Peru campaign, we conducted a Christian Rally for the entire body of Christ in the city. A big push was made, but only 1,200 attended. Immediately following the crusade, we held a Fire Conference. More than 7,000 attended. The press, and all forms of the media, very often herald our message. A crusade gives us a voice in the city.

What about the power of SEED and God's multiplication laws? During a crusade, Gospel seed is sown on a mass scale. His Word will not return unto Him void. Bud Sickler, a sixty year veteran in the mission field of Kenya, once told me this incredible fact. He said, "As far as we can tell there are approximately 20,000 churches in East Africa today as a direct result of T.L. Osborn's crusades." Seed is absolute power.

Pastor Ernesto Banegas comments on the FWO Honduras crusade:

Dear Mike,

I will never be the same. You have showed us how God can use those that dare to believe and obey. I have never seen such a purity of heart, passion for souls, and vision for the nations...

El Progreso has never had such a visitation from Heaven like this crusade that has changed the complete spiritual atmosphere of this city. Religious tradition and superstitious strongholds were broken by the powerful preaching. This was confirmed by the thousands that were saved and healed. Through the demonstration of God's power, the church has gained a credibility and testimony in the city. Many pastors share how their vision was enlarged.

Never before have we seen miracles demonstrated as we did in this crusade. We witnessed God's love towards the world as

He healed the blind, the deaf, the lame, and the lost. Mike Francen brought to El Progreso a REAL and powerful Jesus. Thank you Great God for sending Mike to our city. We will never be the same.

Pastor Ernesto Banegas

Iglesia La Reunion del Senor

Pastor David Sumrall comments on the FWO Manila crusade:

It has been many years that I have begged Mike Francen to come to Manila. His response was always, "we did not need his ministry." It came to the point where I got on my knees in a restaurant. It is harvest time and we need the sickle of the supernatural to shake our generation.

Every generation has the right to see real miracles. Our generation has seen the fake and the exaggerated for far too long. Our generation has almost come to the point where they must choose between dead intellectual religion or the foolishness of the unreal. God, however, still wants the faith of His people to rest on His power and not just words.

I was overwhelmed with the miracles, the intensity of the miracles, the number of the miracles, and the many more we have heard about since the crusade that never made it to the platform to testify. I have never seen such an awesome display of God's goodness, mercy and love. I have been in a lot of crusades, but I have never had the joy to see God work in such an awesome display. The miracles always pointed the people to a decision to repent and accept Christ. We had a conservative count of 20,000 in the baseball stadium by the last night, with over 50,000 different people that came through the services during the meeting. We are still baptizing people in every service from the crusade. This is a crusade with fruit that remains.

I also appreciated the integrity and gentleness Mike and the whole team walked in. They presented a beautiful picture of the ministry of Christ before all the people in their life and ministry.

I pray that they will come back and do an extended meeting with us to shake an entire city.

Pastor David Sumrall

Cathedral of Praise

Chiangrai Crusade Report

We thank God for the crusade in Chiangrai. Many people keep talking about it to this day. It was proved to be very successful. It has brought great changes to churches and to church leaders and non-church people in the community.

As a direct result, new churches have been planted, and more members were added to old churches that were involved in the crusade. Many of those new converts remain in the church to this day.

As an indirect result, unity and right attitudes among the pastors and church leaders of different denominations towards each other is one outstanding blessing. The Christians themselves were inspired and challenged as they saw thousands of people come to the Lord in one meeting and God confirmed the preaching of His Word by healings and miracles. The long time belief among Thai Christians is that winning Thai people to the Lord is so hard because people are so bound to traditions and religion, was proved to be untrue.

We came to realize that healings and miracles are not just history recorded in the Bible, but they can happen even today. The people in the church have caught a 'spirit of evangelism' after the crusade because they know that they too can do the same thing.

People in the church see the importance of presenting the Gospel in a powerful way and it is possible to win as many as hundreds of thousands of souls to the Lord at one time. Therefore, people have become more soul conscious.

Pastor Surapong Prathumwan

Chiangrai Full Gospel Church

I believe in mass crusade evangelism. The book of Acts must be our blueprint for successful ministry. The book of Acts talks of miracles and multitudes. Acts 2:41, Acts 4:4, Acts 8:6, Acts 8:14, Acts 11:21, Acts 14:1, Acts 14:18, Acts 4:19, Acts 14:21, Acts 15:12, Acts 15:30, Acts 17:4, Acts 18:8, Acts 19:10, and so on. Mass crusade evangelism played a key role in the spread of the Gospel in the book of Acts and His story continues today. I believe in mass crusade evangelism.

CHAPTER TWENTY-FOUR

NEVER TOO DEAD FOR A RESURRECTION

A man and woman come together. Through their intimate union a seed is spawned and reaches its pinnacle of success. The colossal miracle of life, on its journey to being birthed into this world, has begun. A seed is planted and a child begins to form.

At the very moment of conception, the child's hair, eye color, and sex has already been determined. At six weeks the fingers begin to form. At eight weeks the eyes, heart, kidneys, and lungs form. At ten weeks it is officially considered a fetus; all parts essential for life have formed.

When my wife was four months pregnant with our daughter, she met me in India. I had been there for some time and when she arrived she brought the ultrasound pictures and videotape of our unborn child. Through the wonders of modern technology, I was able to watch our little girl move, kick, and suck her thumb, four months after conception. It was an awesome sight to watch her tiny heart beating. The seed was coming to maturity. It was growing; she was alive and the beating heart which was pulsating the blood through her little body proved it.

Abortion is one of the great tragedies in our world today.

Some find it within themselves to abort this life and terminate the pregnancy. For a myriad of reasons people have an abortion. Shame, financial pressure, or the unwillingness to accept the responsibility of a child are sound reason for their decision to abort. The reasons for abortion are many. Millions each year reach this fate. Abortion is one of the great tragedies in our world today.

THE GREAT TRAGEDY IN THE CHURCH TODAY

On what could be considered an equal scale, it is the abortion of God-given dreams that plagues the church today. Dreams, given as a child or years ago, work their way into the heart of the child of God. Excitement coupled with the sense of possible fulfillment, grips the heart. A dream is conceived in the heart of the devoted one. It is the abortion of this dream that ranks as one of the great tragedies in the church today.

As I have traveled to numerous churches across America, time and time again I am bombarded with the pain of people's aborted and unfulfilled dreams. Some hear of our mission field adventures, which we have given our lives to and it strikes a chord in their own hearts. Tear-filled eyes have cornered me after many services that confess, "God called me to the nations many years ago. I wish I would have gone." They were seeded with a dream from the throne, yet they aborted that which was given them.

In the past you may have harbored a dream from God to fulfill, with a call placed upon your life. Your dream may not have been one that was calling you to the nations. Maybe your dream was to pastor, sing in the choir, or to become a deacon or an evangelist. Maybe your dream was to become a success in the business world in order to avail vast sums of money to propagate the Gospel. Many dreams and desires may have dropped into your heart. Then for one reason or another, you aborted the God-given dream.

Some abort their dreams because of criticism from their peers. Some abort their dreams because of an overwhelming addiction to obtain material things; or the massive debt of just having. Some quit on their dream because of a spouse or the lack of one; some for lack of financial provision, and others for the lack of direction. For a thousand different reasons people have aborted their dreams.

The slippage of time has left many lying awake in the quietness of their beds with the thoughts of what might have been, and the fulfilled life they might have led, had they continued to pursue the dream. The guilt of the abortion haunts the corners of the mind. The unfulfilled heart is filled with despair. Their aborted dream has affected eternity. Most deem it too late to do anything about it.

The Word of God tells us that we are all part of the body of Christ, fitly joined together.

What if the person who brought you to Christ would have given up on the dream in his or her heart? There is a possibility that you would have never known God's salvation.

The Word of God tells us that we are all part of the body of Christ, fitly joined together. With this realization we must understand that the church can never be all that God intended it to be, without the fulfillment of YOUR dream.

YOU'RE NEVER TOO DEAD FOR A RESURRECTION

John 11:32–44 unveils the potent story of the resurrection of Lazarus.

> Then, when Mary came where Jesus was, and saw Him, she fell down at His feet, saying to Him, "Lord, if You had been here, my brother would not have died."
>
> Therefore, when Jesus saw her weeping, and the Jews who came with her weeping, He groaned in the spirit and was troubled.
>
> And He said, "Where have you laid him?" They said to Him, "Lord, come and see."
>
> Jesus wept.
>
> Then the Jews said, "See how He loved him!" And some of them said, "Could not this Man, who opened the eyes of the blind, also have kept this man from dying?"
>
> Then Jesus, again groaning in Himself, came to the tomb. It was a cave, and a stone lay against it.
>
> Jesus said, "Take away the stone." Martha, the sister of him who was dead, said to Him, "Lord, by this time there is a stench, for he has been dead four days."
>
> Jesus said to her, "Did I not say to you that if you would believe you would see the glory of God?"

Then they took away the stone from the place where the dead man was lying. And Jesus lifted up His eyes and said, "Father, I thank You that You have heard Me. And I know that You always hear Me, but because of the people who are standing by I said this, that they may believe that You sent Me."

Now when He had said these things, He cried with a loud voice, "Lazarus, come forth!"

And he who had died came out bound hand and foot with graveclothes, and his face was wrapped with cloth. Jesus said to them, "Loose him, and let him go."

The majority around decided it was too late. The majority around knew that too much time had passed to fulfill their desire. After all, he had been dead for four days. The body had already been embalmed and the process of decaying had begun to run its course. Surely it was too late.

But then Jesus came. Arrayed in the power of the Spirit, the very presence of God arrived. In the very midst of the majorities' opposition God was saying: YOU'RE NEVER TOO DEAD FOR A RESURRECTION! Thus Lazarus came out of the tomb.

What about your dream that YOU have decided is too late for fulfillment? You, and others around, have decided that too much time has passed. Too many years have heaped themselves against you. "Your dream has no chance of ever being realized," says the majority. God has another opinion. He says, YOU'RE NEVER TOO DEAD FOR A RESURRECTION.

[Abraham] (as it is written, "I HAVE MADE YOU A FATHER OF MANY NATIONS") in the presence of Him whom he believed, even God, who gives life to the dead and calls those things which do not exist as though they did;

who, contrary to hope, in hope believed, so that he became the father of many nations, according to what was spoken, "So shall your descendants be."

And not being weak in faith, he did not consider his own body, already dead (since he was about a hundred years old), and the deadness of Sarah's womb.

He did not waver at the promise of God through unbelief, but was strengthened in faith, giving glory to God, and being fully convinced that what He had promised He was also able to perform.

Romans 4:17-21

They did not consider the deadness. Sarah was at least fifty years past menopause. Natural wisdom says it's too late. God says, YOU'RE NEVER TOO DEAD FOR A RESURRECTION!

RESURRECTION POWER TODAY

In the nation of India we were conducting another one of our mass campaigns. One night in the Hubli crusade as I was preaching, a great deal of excitement and commotion was transpiring just off the right side of the platform. My wife and crusade director were there, and I turned to inquire as to what was happening.

I was preaching on the subject, "The power of the Lord was present to heal" and while I did, HE DID. A little seven year old girl was a recipient of the Master's touch. The cause of the commotion was this seven year old girl was walking towards the platform carrying an offering. The excitement was that this petite Indian girl had NEVER stood or walked before in her life! Contracting polio as an infant, the dreaded disease left her legs totally dead and useless. Seven years of deadness in her legs had to give way to the resurrection power of God. YOU'RE NEVER TOO DEAD FOR A RESURRECTION!

In another campaign in Liberia, West Africa, a twenty-one year old woman attended. She also had contracted polio as an infant. She came to our Monrovia crusade adorned with what the Africans call an "iron shoe." The apparatus entangled her legs with metal and leather. A special shoe was attached to the end of the cumbersome braces enabling her to stand.

For twenty-one years her legs were dead. Medical science had no formulas to revive them. There was no hope of recovery. During the crusade the presence of Christ filled the stadium. A divine touch from above was realized and she immediately began to un-strap the braces from her legs. Holding those heavy braces high over head, she stormed to the platform for all to see. Walking on limbs once thought too dead to ever function, glory was given to God. YOU'RE NEVER TOO DEAD FOR A RESURRECTION!

That same resurrection power is available to you now. It is available to bring life to dead dreams.

RESURRECTION POWER FOR ME

At nineteen I accepted Christ, and in a matter of weeks I received the call of God to go to the nations. I knew I must give my life for the cause of Christ.

At that stage in my life I was extremely shy and backwards. Up to that point I had devoted my life and every waking moment to basketball. I played it well, and I knew it well.

In high school each student was required to take certain English courses. In one of these classes I was required to give a two minute speech on the subject of my choice. I chose basketball, thinking I could talk for at least two minutes on something I played eight hours every day.

The big day came. As I began, my heart raced and my throat tightened to the point of strangulation. I sat down, unable to finish the two minutes.

My hair was long and the bangs covered my eyes in an attempt to hide from the world. I was afraid to talk to people. A friend invited me over to his parents' home for dinner one night. He shared with them my call to be an evangelist to the world. I sat in the corner of the room, as was my custom, and said nothing. When I left the room his mother said, "Mike will never be an evangelist; he has deep psychological problems. Give him the name of this psychiatrist."

People began to extinguish the dream and fire within my heart. A church I worked with told me I was too young, didn't have enough experience, and did not know how to praise and worship properly. They were less than enthusiastic about my dream. I asked the pastor of the church to ordain me into the ministry. He responded by saying, "We don't do that anymore."

He informed me of this on a Thursday. That Sunday I felt crushed as he proceeded to ordain the youth pastor and children's pastor into the ministry.

I began the abortion process of my dream. People I respected began to cast their shadows of doubt over my dream. Bombarded from all sides, I began to form a mental picture of a small house I would buy, a nice family I would settle down with, and a form of job and ministry I might adapt to. I began to abort the God-given dream.

YOU'RE GONNA DO IT

A short time after this I found myself in Nigeria with Dr. Benson Idahosa. Christ came to me with resurrection life. For nearly three weeks the Spirit of God would wake me as I slept. A resounding, "Your gift will make a way for you" penetrated my ears and permeated my being. Day and night for weeks it rang loud in my ears.

While there, I had the privilege of meeting T.L. Osborn. He laid his hands on me and prayed. After that he looked deeply into my eyes and said, "You're gonna do it, you're gonna do it, you're gonna do it."

I intensely watched Benson and Jerry Savelle conduct massive crusades. Miracles swept across the huge fields of people. Night after night in those meetings a whirlwind spun above my head that said, "You can do this!"

The Spirit of God met me. Resurrection life came to the dreams that I had let fall by the wayside. I left Nigeria with my dream restored, a fire ignited, and a determination to never let anyone talk me out of my call for His glory.

Today I am living my dream. I have had the honor of seeing literally millions of people come to Christ as I have stood before audiences in excess of 300,000 people. YOUR DREAM IS NEVER TOO DEAD FOR A RESURRECTION!

- Never rewrite your theology to accommodate a tragedy.
- God never consults your past to determine your future.
- Rejection is not fatal, it is merely someone else's opinion.
- You can only conquer your past by focusing on your future.
- You must harbor a passion to champion a cause

IT'S TIME TO DREAM AGAIN!

CHAPTER TWENTY-FIVE

HIGH TREASON

Then God said, "Let Us make man in Our image, according to Our likeness: let them have dominion over the fish of the sea, over the birds of the air, and over the cattle, over all the earth and over every creeping thing that creeps on the earth."

So God created man in His own image; in the image of God He created him, male and female He created them.

Then God blessed them, and God said to them, "Be fruitful and multiply; fill the earth and subdue it; have dominion...."

Genesis 1:26–28

It was always God's intention for man to have authority and dominion over the earth. He created mankind in His likeness to rule and reign over everything on the earth.

In Psalm 8:4–6 we read:

What is man that You are mindful of him, And the son of man that You visit him?

For You have made him a little lower than the angels, And you have crowned him with glory and honor.

You have made him to have dominion over the
works of Your hands; You have put all things under
his feet.

Man was created with a crown of glory that was placed upon
his head by the heavenly Creator. This crown of glory symbolized
the authority God had given to man.

The writer of Hebrews further substantiates the Psalmist's
claim, quoting:

What is man that You are mindful of him, or the son
of man that You take care of him?

You made him a little lower than the angels; You
crowned him with glory and honor, and set him
over the works of Your hands.

You have put all things in subjection under his feet.
For in that He put all in subjection under him, He
left nothing that is not put under him....

Hebrews 2:6–8

Man was created to have dominion! The word "dominion"
means "to prevail against, or to rule or reign." Therefore, man was
created to rule and reign over all the creations of God. He was to
rule over everything that "creeps on the earth."

That even included the devil! We were created not to fear the
devil, but to rule and reign over him. That was God's original
intention.

God had given Adam all authority and dominion on the earth. He
told him to protect and preserve His kingdom from any intruders.

> Then the Lord God took the man and put him in the
> garden of Eden to tend and keep it.

Genesis 2:15

Man was told to keep the garden. The word "keep" means "to guard, protect, and defend." Adam was supposed to protect the garden from any intruders. This was not an unfair task required by God, because Adam had the ability to do so—he had all dominion on the earth.

The problem was, Adam did not keep the intruder out! The authority and dominion that was given to man was Adam's as long as he retained and used it. It was by sin, therefore, that Adam surrendered his authority.

> So when the woman saw that the tree was good for
> food, that it was pleasant to the eyes, and a tree desir-
> able to make one wise, she took of its fruit and ate.
> She also gave to her husband with her, and he ate.

Genesis 3:6

The very moment Adam yielded to the sin of his wife, he committed high treason—he sold out to the devil. Adam was not deceived, according to First Timothy 2:14; Adam knowingly and willingly sinned against God. At the moment he sinned, *Adam conferred all authority and dominion he had to Satan by default.*

Man fell completely: body, soul, and spirit. In doing so, he instantly lost dominion over evil and disease. Satan, at that moment, became "the god of this world." (See II Corinthians 4:4)

Jesus recognized Satan's rightful claim to dominion. Immediately after Jesus' baptism, the Spirit of God led Him into the wilderness for 40 days of prayer and fasting. After those 40 days, the devil came to Him to tempt Him.

> Then the devil, taking Him up on a high mountain, showed Him all the kingdoms of the world in a moment of time.
>
> And the devil said to Him, "All this authority I will give You, and their glory; for this has been delivered to me, and I give it to whomever I wish."
>
> Luke 4:5-6

In order for this to be a true temptation, Satan would have to be able to deliver what he said. How could Satan fill such a tall order, and how did he inherit all of the authority?

Dominion over the kingdoms of the earth, which once belonged to man, was delivered to Satan at the fall of man.

Notice Satan told Jesus in verse 6, *"All this authority I will give You...for this has been delivered to me..."*

Who delivered all of the authority to Satan? We know that God would never give Satan dominion. Dominion over the kingdoms of the earth, which once belonged to man, was delivered to Satan at the fall of man. Satan, like Adam, then had the right to confer that authority on anyone he wanted.

That is exactly what Adam had already done. Adam had delivered that authority to Satan.

Jesus called Satan *"the prince of this world"* (John 14:30). However, I thank God He was not willing to leave us in that fallen state. God had a plan.

CHAPTER TWENTY-SIX

SATAN, A DEFEATED FOE

Many books have been written and many sermons preached on Satan and his kingdom of darkness. I am convinced, however, that there are really only two things we need to know about the devil: First, he is a liar; and, second, he is defeated!

God was not willing to leave His creation in the fallen state brought on by Adam. His Father's heart could not allow man to live forever under the rule of the devil. Immediately after the fall of man, God put His plan into action to restore fellowship and dominion back to mankind. His plan was Jesus.

> **And I will put enmity between you and the woman, and between your seed and her Seed; He shall bruise your head, and you shall bruise His heel.**
>
> **Genesis 3:15**

The big love plan was Jesus! He was to bring us redemption.

For since by man [Adam] came death, [including lost authority] by Man [Jesus] also came the resurrection of the dead.

> **For as in Adam all die, even so in Christ all shall be made alive.**
>
> **I Corinthians 15:21-22**

The purpose behind the incarnation of Christ was so that man might be given the right to become a child of God.

> *The purpose behind the incarnation of Christ was so that man might be given the right to become a child of God.*

Man would only be able to receive eternal life after he had been legally redeemed (or bought back) from Satan's authority. We have been purchased with blood—the blood of Jesus Christ!

That was God's love plan. His desire was to restore mankind to fellowship and to restore authority to the place He had originally intended it to be.

Through Jesus, we have redemption. It was through His death, burial, and resurrection that restoration of authority has come back to mankind.

> **Having disarmed principalities and powers, He made a public spectacle of them, triumphing over them in it.**
>
> **Colossians 2:15**

Satan has been defeated! He has been stripped of his power, and the authority he once had was taken away from him. The devil no longer has dominion on this earth, except what we allow him to have. Redemption has given it back to you and me as children of God.

He has delivered us from the power of darkness and translated us into the kingdom of the Son of His love, in whom we have redemption through His blood....

Colossians 1:13-14

In as much then as the children have partaken of flesh and blood, He Himself likewise shared in the same, that through death He might destroy him who had the power of death, that is, the devil; and release those through fear of death were all their lifetime subject to bondage.

Hebrews 2:14-15

Jesus brought to naught the hosts of hell! He stripped them of authority, and He rendered the devil and all the demons in hell powerless.

Jesus said to the apostle John on the Isle of Patmos:

I am He who lives, and was dead, and behold, I am alive forevermore. Amen. And I have the keys of Hades and of Death.

Revelation 1:18

Satan was stripped of the authority he once possessed. Keys represent authority. Jesus now has them. He did not conquer Satan for Himself; He conquered Satan for you and me.

As F.F. Bosworth once said, *"You can become a devil master overnight."* How is this possible? By understanding the defeated devil and our restored authority.

Jesus eternally defeated Satan, not for Himself; but, rather for mankind. His victory over the devil was a substitutionary act. What that means is that Jesus' victory is our victory. All He did in triumphing over the devil He did as a substitute for you and me.

Satan was stripped of the authority he once possessed.

Before Jesus ascended to be with the Father, He said:

> **All authority has been given to Me in heaven and on earth. Go therefore....**
>
> Matthew 28:18–19

Jesus, before ascending back to the Father, conferred (delegated) His authority on the earth to His church. We are the Body of Christ. When Jesus ascended on high as the head of the Body,

> **He [God] put all things under His [Jesus] feet, and gave Him to be head over all things to the church, which is His body, the fullness of him who fills all in all.**
>
> Ephesians 1:22–23

Mark's account of this delegation of authority declares that Jesus said:

> **And these signs will follow those who believe: In My name they will cast out demons; they will speak with new tongues;**

They will take up serpents; and if they drink anything deadly, it will by no means hurt them; they will
lay hands on the sick, and they will recover.

Mark 16:17-18

Jesus has restored dominion and authority back to His church.
The child of God has been given back the authority that was lost
in the Garden of Eden. You can reign in life!

CHAPTER TWENTY-SEVEN

SEPARATE YOURSELF

Days of preparation are never wasted days. As the call of God

> *Days of preparation are never wasted days.*

burns within the heart of man, an overwhelming desire to "go" can sometimes cloud better judgment and His timing. Jesus had thirty years of preparation time before He entered into His earthly ministry. Ecclesiastes chapter 3 tells us there is a time for everything.

Too often we see the aftermath of an unprepared life. When God places the call on a life, certain gifts and anointings are bestowed. The Bible says, *"A man's gift maketh room for him, and bringeth him before great men"* (Proverbs 18:16). We see the "gift" quickly cause some to rise to great heights of ministry. We see many of those fall just as quickly as they rose. A man's gift can sometimes take him to a place where his character cannot keep him. Integrity is the ONLY thing you possess that no one can take away from you. People can steal your joy, money, or any material possession you have. Your ministry, health, or family can be taken away in a moments time. No one can take away your integrity. This must be given up by a conscious choice of an individual. Integrity issues rarely constitute major decisions made before a congregation. It is the hidden matters of the heart, the "little things" done, or not done, in the privacy of your own world. This is where integrity takes center stage.

Count on a period of preparation in your life. The Spirit of God will put you on the Potter's wheel to shape you into a vessel fit for the Master's use. The roadsides are lined with ministries who were never properly prepared. Character, resolve, and integrity are developed, not bestowed. These foundational pillars are forged over time and days of preparation.

WHO INVITED LOT?

Now the LORD had said to Abram: "Get thee out of thy country, and from thy kindred, and from thy father's house, unto a land that I will show thee: And I wilt make of thee a great nation, and I will bless thee, and make thy name great; and thou shalt be a blessing: And I will bless them that bless thee, and curse him that curseth thee: and in thee shall all families of the earth be blessed. So Abram departed as the LORD had spoken to him, and Lot went with him... Then Abram went up from Egypt, he and his wife and all that he had, and Lot with him..." Lot also, who went with Abram, had flocks and herds and tents. Now the land was not able to support them, that they might dwell together, for their possessions were so great that they could not dwell together.

And there was strife between the herdsmen of Abram's livestock and the herdsmen of Lot's livestock... So Abram said to Lot, "Please separate from me."

And the LORD said to Abram, after Lot had separated from him:"Lift your eyes now and look from the place where you are—northward, southward, eastward, and westward; for all the land which you see I give to you and your descendants forever."

Gen. 12:1-5, 13:6-7,14-15

Who invited Lot? God made it very clear that Abram was to separate himself, but Lot tagged along. It was not until Lot left that God brought Abram into His fullness. There are few pioneers, few who dare to actually pursue a dream, and few who make the sacrifice of this present life to fulfill the call. There are few who fall into this category, but there are many who would like to "come along for the ride." Sometimes there MUST be a parting of ways to fulfill the call.

Often there must be a separation from ties that bind as God prepares you for ministry. He desires to bring you to a new and higher place, while some past relationships only lie in wait to sabotage those who dare to succeed.

As Jesus called His disciples, every one of them had to make a decision to separate himself. Then Peter began to say to Him, "See, we have left all and followed You!"

So Jesus answered and said, "Assuredly, I say to you, there is no one who has left house or brothers or sisters or father or mother or wife or children or lands, for My sake and the gospel's, who shall not receive a hundred-fold now in this time—houses and brothers and sisters and mothers and children and lands, with persecutions—and in the age to come, eternal life."

Mark 10:28-30

As they ministered to the Lord and fasted, the Holy Spirit said, "Now separate to Me Barnabas and Saul for the work to which I have called them!"

Acts 13:2

God is calling you to make tough decisions and separate yourself from people who would minimize your life. God has brought you to a place and requires you to separate yourself from: old doctrines, old ideas, old methods, old practices, and old prayers.

Everybody needs a hero. Pick your teachers carefully.

It is a form of insanity to continue to do the same things over and over, and then think you will get different results.

But imitate those who through faith and patience inherit the promises.

Hebrews 6:12

Everybody needs a hero. Pick your teachers carefully. The Bible says when you are fully taught you will be like your teacher. (Luke 6:40)

FIVE SUCCESS PRINCIPLES

ONE: Think (dream) big enough for God to fit into your thoughts. Jesus said to his disciples, *"Go into all the world..."* They had never been anywhere. Vision will always stretch the very fiber of your being. Its cause will take you out of yourself into another self that is greater.

If your dreams match your bank account you are on your own. Allow your dreams to match God's bank account.

Pastors ask me if there is anything wrong in having a small church. I tell them, "No, not for a week." "But God is not into numbers, numbers are just not important," they reply. Yet, the Bible talks much of numbers. Jesus had twelve disciples, there were twelve in the upper room and He fed the five thousand. Peter saw three thousand come to Christ on the day of Pentecost. Daily, He added to the church and the church multiplied. God even has a book called Numbers. Jesus Himself said several times, "Nevertheless." Have a dream that will inspire others.

TWO: Make the decisions today that will create the desired future. Jesus said, *"Follow me and I will make you..."* (Matt 4:19) Understand it is not only the major decisions that shape your destiny, but the little habits we form which build the character of the person that weighs heavily into our future. Losers make decisions that create a desired present. Champions make decisions that create a desired future.

THREE: Make a plan. Build by the plan, not plan by the building. Science tells us that a person has 2,000 ideas a day. If you cannot verbalize your dream, you cannot realize it. Always use biblical principles as your blueprint for success. Talk with God about your dreams and wisely share it with others. People will do all they can to discourage your daring faith and endeavors to realize it. Do not share your 16x20 ideas with 3x5 minds.

FOUR: Set goals. Make yourself work with a time factor. If you never set any goals you will wake up one day white headed—still dreaming.

FIVE: Determine never to quit. I once asked Lester Sumrall, who celebrated more than sixty years of successful ministry, "What is one of the great keys to success in ministry?" He was quick to respond, "Just don't quit." Your dream is worth it. Do not pursue a dream that does not consume you. If you do not quit—YOU WIN.

Resolve brings the fortitude to help you finish. Cortez was a cruel man, but his means of convincing his soldiers to conquer the Aztecs after they had landed in Mexico proved to be most effective. As the men stood at attention on the beach, Cortez ordered that the ships they had just arrived on to be burned and sunk. There would be no going back to Spain.

Before you have one thought of retreating from the dreams you seek, burn the boats that would float you back into a nominal Christian existence.

Why should I agree with someone else's standards? Why must I adopt another's definition of success? Vision allows me to write my own ticket and determine my own destination.

CHAPTER TWENTY-EIGHT

ALL THINGS ARE YOURS

Therefore let no one boast in men. For all things are yours: whether Paul or Apollos or Cephas, or the world or life or death, or things present or things to come—all are yours.

I Corinthians 3:21-22

This text knows no limits, it has no boundaries. Claim everything, exclude nothing—for ALL things are yours.

So often life is so meager when it could have been so magnificent; so sorry when it could have been so significant; so futile when it could have been so full; and so paltry when God meant it to be so powerful. It is time to take possession of, and responsibility for, the entire world.

This portion of Scripture must have sounded absurd and far-fetched to those early Corinthians. After all there was no royalty among them, no one of lofty pedigree, no stars, or none of political importance. They were most ordinary.

God looked at those people and said, "ALL THINGS ARE YOURS!" He looks at you right now, regardless of what your inventory tells you and says, "All things are yours."

The past is yours—learn from it. The present is yours—fulfill it. The future is yours—decide it. The Bible is yours—know it. The

Gospel is yours—preach it. Cancer is yours—cure it. The heathen are yours—claim it. Sickness is yours—heal it. The earth is yours—enhance it. Time is yours—use it. War is yours—stop it. Death is yours—delay it. Opportunity is yours—seize it. Eternal life is yours—lay hold of it. Heaven is yours—meet me there! ALL THINGS ARE YOURS.

...make plans. Don't take care, take charge.

You are the sons and daughters of God. There is no mountain too big! Don't make excuses, make plans. Don't take care, take charge.

God has given you everything you will ever need to be successful in ministry today.

QUALIFIED BY GOD

> Now when the Sabbath was past, Mary Magdalene, Mary the mother of James, and Salome bought spices, that they might come and anoint Him. Very early in the morning, on the first day of the week, they came to the tomb when the sun was risen. And they said among themselves, "Who will roll away the stone from the door of the tomb for us?" But when they looked up, they saw that the stone had been rolled away—for it was very large. And entering the tomb, they saw a young man clothed in a long white robe sitting on the right side; and they were alarmed. But he said to them, "Do not be alarmed.

You seek Jesus of Nazareth, who was crucified. He is risen! He is not here. See the place where they laid him. But go and tell His disciples,—AND PETER— that He is going before you into Galilee; there you will see Him, as He said to you!"

Mark 16:1-7

AND PETER. The other disciples were not mentioned by name, but Peter was. In Matthew 14, Jesus rebuked Peter for a lack of faith. In Matthew 16, Peter received revelation of Christ's divinity, then moments later he was rebuked as the devil spoke through him. In Matthew 26, the bold disciple denied even knowing Jesus before a simple peasant girl.

It's as if all of heaven watched Peter fall, and it is as if all of heaven wanted him to get back up again. Heaven wanted Peter to know he did not fall beyond the love of God. Heaven wanted Peter to know that he was not going to be left out. It's not everyday you'll find someone to give you a second chance, much less someone who will give you a second chance everyday.

"Don't live with the dogs."

There are not many second chances afforded us in the world today. The press lies in wait for another minister to stumble. So-called friends almost gloat with a "I knew it" attitude when we fall. In this dog eat dog world, Jesus would say, "Don't live with the dogs."

Jesus never consults your past to determine your future. God does not disqualify you for service; don't disqualify yourself.

CHAPTER TWENTY-NINE

THE GOOD NEWS GOSPEL

Some time ago I was in Bogota, Columbia with T.L. Osborn. In one of our conversations he made a statement that I have pondered often since that time. He said, *"Charismatics today preach faith, destroy hope, and ignore love."*

With a ramrod fervency we thrust the word of faith message upon hungry hearers. If things do not happen according to our predetermined ideology of the way God fulfills His promise, accusations of doubt and unbelief are hurled towards them. Often times hope is destroyed as they feel they cannot attain the level of faith needed. Love is nowhere to be found.

I understand the word of faith message, I am a faith preacher. But faith must be bathed within the confines of hope and love. It is love that will open a person's heart so that they might receive. Sometimes, in ministry, all you can give

> *God never called us to change the world, He called us to love the world.*

is a ray of hope, but understand that hope is the very foundation of faith.

GOD NEVER CALLED US TO CHANGE THE WORLD, HE CALLED US TO LOVE THE WORLD. The moment I think I've got to change you, then I must find fault with you. I will have to come and find out everything that is wrong with you and magnify it, because I think I have to change you. But if I come to love you I have to accept you just the way you are. And the love of God supersedes everything else. If we love them, we will win them to His cause. Then God will change them.

A HEAVENLY PERSPECTIVE

It is time we see from a heavenly perspective. We have been conditioned to react and respond from what we see on the outside. We look at a vile sinner, or an opposing atheist and withdraw with an attitude, "You'll get yours" as we curse the very ground on which they walk. Seeing through the eyes of Christ, a new world of possibilities unveils itself.

If we could see the world of people in the light of the Gospel, our attitudes would be drastically altered. Mark 5:1–20 says:

> Then they came to the other side of the sea, to the country of the Gadarenes. And when He had come out of the boat, immediately there met Him out of the tombs a man with an unclean spirit, who had his dwelling among the tombs; and no one could bind him, not even with chains, because he had often been bound with shackles and chains. And the chains had been pulled apart by him, and the shackles broken in pieces; neither could anyone tame him. And always, night and day, he was in the

mountains and in the tombs, crying out and cutting himself with stones.

When he saw Jesus from afar, he ran and worshiped Him. And he cried out with a loud voice and said, "What have I to do with You, Jesus, Son of the Most High God? I implore You by God that You do not torment me."

For He said to him, "Come out of the man, unclean spirit!" Then He asked him, "What is your name?"

And he answered saying, "My name is Legion; for we are many." Also he begged Him earnestly that He would not send them out of the country.

Now a large herd of swine was feeding there near the mountains. So all the demons begged Him, saying, "Send us to the swine, that we may enter them." And at once Jesus gave them permission. Then the unclean spirits went out and entered the swine (there were about two thousand); and the herd ran violently down the steep place into the sea, and drowned in the sea.

So those who fed the swine fled, and they told it in the city and in the country. And they went out to see what it was that had happened. Then they came to Jesus, and saw the one who had been demon-possessed and had the legion, sitting and clothed and in his right mind. And they were afraid. And those who saw it told them how it happened to him who had been demon-possessed, and about the swine. Then they began to plead with Him to depart from their region.

And when He got into the boat, he who had been demon-possessed begged Him that he might be with Him. However, Jesus did not permit him, but said to him, "Go home to your friends, and tell them what great things the Lord has done for you, and how He has had compassion on you." And he departed and began to proclaim in Decapolis (ten cities) all that Jesus had done for him, and all marveled.

Jesus looked at the demon possessed man and saw a man with a call on his life to bring the Gospel to ten cities. In his dire despair, a call of God still rested upon his life. A heavenly perspective forces us to see a man with ten cities waiting for his message.

Jesus said to the man: "Go (the mission and commission) home to your friends, and tell (the mandate) them what great things the Lord has done for you (the message), and how He has had compassion (the motive—love) on you. And he departed and began to proclaim in Decapolis (the multitudes, ten cities) all that Jesus had done for him; and all marveled (the miracle)."

Mark 5:19-20

GOOD NEWS ANOINTING

Many today ascribe "special" gifts to my life. They proclaim I have been given the "gift of healing" or a "unique anointing" of miracles for those that are crippled or deaf. The numerous and various miracles which take place in our crusades send the religious on a search to explain why we have such manifestations.

I have witnessed scores of miracles take place in our campaigns. My eyes have beheld the wonder and beauty of those who were born crippled, now taking their first steps in twenty years. I have marveled at those who uttered their first words from our crusade platform even though they were born deaf and dumb eighteen years earlier.

In massive open fields I have seen seas of humanity gather and whole-heartedly accept Jesus Christ, as they renounced their dead gods. I have been honored and humbled to lead millions of people into the Kingdom of God.

I am a proclaimer of Truth.

I have never claimed to have a "unique anointing" or "special gift." I am a proclaimer of Truth. I preach the GOSPEL. Herein lies the secret of success and power in ministry.

> I am not ashamed of the GOSPEL of Christ, for it is the power of God...
>
> Rom. 1:16

ANOTHER JESUS

> But I fear, lest somehow, as the serpent deceived Eve by his craftiness, so your minds may be corrupted from the simplicity that is in Christ. For if he who comes preaches ANOTHER JESUS whom we have

not preached, or if you receive a different spirit which you have not received, or a DIFFERENT GOSPEL which you have not accepted...

2 Corinthians 11:3-4

What is the Gospel? The message is 1) God's creation, 2) Satan's destruction, 3) Christ's redemption, and 4) Our restoration. The presentation of this brings life and hope to a hurting world.

Young and daring in faith, the excitement of new found truths in the Word of God causes us to boldly step out. Commanding spirits, laying hands on the sick, and proclaiming liberty to the captives is a totally acceptable lifestyle. After all it is His Word. That is the Gospel we believe. That is the Jesus we talk about.

Too often apparent disappointments cause men and women of God to withdraw. Prayer for the sick is offered, but nothing happened. Before long another Jesus is being presented. Another Gospel is being preached. Suddenly the message changes from "God will heal and deliver you. It is part of His salvation," to "healing is a divine act of God, not to be expected but rather accepted if He happens to bring it your way."

Proclaim the Gospel (Good News) with boldness and authority. Bathed in love it will win the hearts of the world. I am not ashamed of the Gospel of Christ, for it IS the power of God...

CHAPTER THIRTY

THE FUTURE IS MY FRIEND

The past is our teacher, the present our opportunity, and the future is our friend. People relish the past. At the turn of the century the impact of the great Welsh and Azusa street revivals swept across the world. In the 40's and 50's a healing revival caused huge tents and auditoriums to be filled to capacity. Today, people long for the return of the old. We are chained to the past, too often limited to barriers and borders of our forefathers. Let us learn from the past, at the same time avoid being bound to it. God says, *"Behold, I will do a new thing"* (Isaiah 43:18).

Incredible opportunities avail themselves to us in an ongoing basis.

Incredible opportunities avail themselves to us in an ongoing basis. Often a quick inventory of past experiences, failures, and our present level of limited knowledge forces us to unconsciously pass them by. The gauntlet echoes in our ears that says, "I tried that before." "It's never been done." "I'm too old."

The *past*. Some despise it as they do their best to ignore, deny, or forget it. Others fear the future, so they continue soul-ties to the days gone by.

I understand the Apostle Paul's purpose when He penned, *"Brethren, I do not count myself to have apprehended; but one thing [I do], forgetting those things which are behind and reaching forward to those things which are ahead"* (Philippians 3:13). I also perceive the potent power in reflecting on past victories. Looking to the past, we can find motivation for the future. An inventory of triumphs from the past encourages us to seize the future with faith and confidence.

As a shepherd boy, David stood before Saul begging for a shot at the giant. King Saul looked upon David's youth, slight build, and inexperience, and determined he had NO chance.

1 Samuel 17:34–36 records David's response, *"But David said to Saul, 'Your servant used to keep his father's sheep, and when a lion or a bear came and took a lamb out of the flock, I went out after it and struck it, and delivered [the lamb] from its mouth; and when it arose against me, I caught [it] by its beard, and struck and killed it. Your servant has killed both lion and bear; and this uncircumcised Philistine will be like one of them, seeing he has defied the armies of the living God.'"*

David looked back to previous victories and captured motivation and faith for the task at hand. He remembered God's hand with him as he battled the bear. He smiled as his mind replayed the victory over the lion. With courage and faith, he would face a new foe. Undaunted, he claimed yet another victory. Looking to the past, he found motivation for the future.

> Now therefore, thus shall you say to My servant David, "Thus says the LORD of hosts: 'I took you from the sheepfold, from following the sheep, to be ruler

over My people Israel. And I have been with you wherever you have gone, and have cut off all your enemies from before you, and have made you a name like the name of the great men who [are] on the earth.'"

1 Chronicles 17:7–8

THE BULLET PROOF WASHINGTON

In the book entitled, *The Bulletproof George Washington*, the author David Barton expounds on a great battle which took place in 1755 between the French and British for supremacy in America. The French had purposed to divide America as they joined with the native Indian forces. The Brits sent the highly decorated General Braddock, who was well versed in European warfare.

Upon Braddock's arrival, he summoned for a young colonel by the name of George Washington. Alongside Braddock, Washington would ride and battle for the strategic position and control of Fort Duquense. The battle would be fierce.

Washington's mother heard of the upcoming battle, and begged her son not to go as she feared for his life. Colonel Washington wrote this letter back to his mom:

"The God to whom you commended me, madam, when I set out upon a more perilous errand, defended me from all harm, I TRUST HE WILL DO SO NOW. Do not you?" (pg.23)

Looking to the past, Washington found motivation for the future. The young Washington went to battle with faith and confidence in God.

The Indians were known as unerring marksmen. Their ambush style of fighting decimated 1,300 of Braddock's troops. Every mounted officer (63 of them) was slain, except Washington. Following the battle, the Indians testified they had singled him out and repeatedly shot at him. They were convinced he was protected by invisible power and that no bullet could harm him. Two horses were shot out from underneath him. Four bullets had ripped through his clothes. Yet, none of his blood spilled.

One famous Indian warrior testified, *"Washington was never born to be killed by a bullet! I had seventeen fair fires at him with my rifle, and after all could not bring him to the ground."* (pg. 49)*

Indian Chief Red Hawk personally shot eleven times at the young colonel. At that point, he quit because his gun had never before missed its mark. He was convinced the Great Spirit had protected Washington.

Thirteen years after that great battle, Chief Red Hawk met Washington and said, *"I have come to pay homage to the man who is the particular favorite of Heaven, and who can never die in battle."* (pg 51)

Forget past defeats. Do not dwell on mishaps which may have devastated you for a season. Let your confidence not rest in education, talent, or personal abilities. Let those things become a faded memory. But you can reflect on past victories and find confidence for your future.

Many times I have embarked upon a new country. As we prepare for another mass miracle crusade, doubt and unbelief manifest itself in the form of a well-meaning pastor or missionary.

---

*Barton, David, The Bullet Proof George Washington
(Aledo, TX.:WallBuilder Press, 1990).

"It is different here. Don't expect the same results here as you have had in other places," they say. Witchdoctors hurl their curses as they spread their jujus around the crusade site.

I know that in and of myself, I have nothing to give. But acting as His Ambassador, I have a message of hope, a word of life, and a proclamation of healing and deliverance. The Word never fails. Hundreds of times I have stood on crude wooden platforms as crowds of more than 150,000 people have gathered. NEVER once was there a failure of God to confirm His Word. I stand every time now with confidence. I can look to the past and find motivation for the future. He never fails!

ARMED & DANGEROUS

> And it shall come to pass afterward that I will pour out My Spirit on all flesh; your sons and your daughters shall prophesy, your old men shall dream dreams, your young men shall see visions. And also on My menservants and on My maidservants I will pour out my Spirit in those days.
>
> Joel 2:28-29

This potent portion of Scripture reveals four different groups of people. The first group addresses the daughters along with the sons. Society and often times the church has done its best to bind the potential of women today. "Sit down and be silent" resounds through the fabric of the world in which we live in. The ladies are told from a very young age, "It's a man's world."

What does Joel 2:28 tell the women, when the world around them says be silent? God says, "I'm going to give you a voice."

The next group mentioned here is the old. When the hair turns gray and the face begins to wrinkle, society gives the elderly a pension and a rocking chair, and tells them to relax in their final days. They are told their ideas are outdated and its time to make room for the young fire-brands. God looks at these same people and says, "I am going to give you a dream again." People may say you are too old. Who said a calendar had anything to do with it?

At eighty years of age, Moses led three and a half million people out of captivity. Caleb at eighty-five took God at His word and said, "Give me that mountain." Colonel Sanders was seventy years old when he introduced Kentucky Fried Chicken into the world. Ray Kroc, at seventy years old, invented the Big Mac. Picasso, at eighty-eight years old, was still painting priceless pieces of art. At eighty-five, Thomas Edison invented the mimeograph machine. And John Wesley as an eighty-eight year old was still traveling on horseback shaking the nations. The old have a tendency to look at the sunset, rather than the sunrise. A calendar has nothing to do with it. It is time for the old man or woman to dream again.

The old have a tendency to look at the sunset, rather than the sunrise.

Next, this passage addresses the young man. He hears time and time again he has NO EXPERIENCE. God says, *"Your young men shall see visions."* He will give the young authority and influence in the day of his youth. He will shape his generation.

God saw fit to make an eight year old, Josiah, the king and ruler of His people. Obviously, God does not look at a calendar to decide if the vessel is the proper age for the task at hand.

The final group covered in these verses are the menservants and maidservants—the common people. The common people have always been made to feel as if they are just passed over. The wealthy and influential have governed the ways of the masses, even in the church. God looks at these people and says, "I am going to pour out my Spirit upon them." He is going to give the common folk a vote, and they will make a difference!

Depicted throughout the Word of God, are the vessels who were recipients of the outpouring of God's Spirit. Portrayed are the Elijahs who confronted and brought to naught the prophets of Baal, the Davids who slew the giant, the Pauls who raised the dead, and the Peters who brought thousands to Christ. I'm not talking about a revolution, but a revelation of who you are in Christ.

We can look at the Scriptures and forge our future with anticipation, vision, and the determination to fulfill the God-given dreams which can bring us to the destination God desires.

This is God's opinion. When man attempts to create the ties that bind, God has His own idea. The future IS my friend, for God is on my side.